D1193928

"It's a Very Simple Game"

The Life & Times of Charley Eckman

Charley Eckman & Fred Neil

Printed in the United States of America

ISBN # 1-880325-15-2

Library of Congress # 95-83-142

Cover illustration by Jack Davy

Jacket design, page design & typesetting by Susan Shugars,
RPI Marketing Communications
7929 Liberty Road
Baltimore, Maryland 21244
(410) 655-8858

"It's a Very Simple Game"

The Life & Times of Charley Eckman

Charley Eckman & Fred Neil

BORDERLANDS PRESS
Baltimore ❑ 1995

This book is dedicated to our families,
past, present and future.

Acknowledgments

The authors express deep appreciation to Debbie Bean who transcribed the interview tapes; Hal Grossman, Seymour Smith, and Linda Eckman Watts for material that enhanced this book; and a group of individuals who have provided support and encouragement: Carol Allen, Brian Applestein, Dr. Phil Block, Ellsworth Boyd, Ron Davis, Debbie Estes Grosvenor, Bob Gunther, Ted Kunkel, John Murphy, Jay Neil, Paul Paolisso, Chip Reed, Tom Scheurich, and legal advisor Gail Neil. A special thanks to Charley's wonderful family — Wilma, Barry, Linda, Gail and Janet who provided us with insight, guidance and much more.

Table of Contents

Foreword

by Tom Clancy

Charley Eckman will probably never be as famous as he ought to be. Partly that results from having been born in the wrong place, and part results from being loyal to it—for much the same reason that Henry Louis Menken was loyal to the Baltimore area; it's not a bad place to live, even though it never seems to garner the attention of places like New York. I suppose bombast does count for something.

Charley is what some call a media personality—the other term, for those who don't regularly travel the airwaves, is "character." He's all of that, and he's a man who knows his sports.

Charley isn't so much irreverent as direct. One is rarely in doubt of his opinion of anything, and his diction is not polluted with circumlocutions. He says what he thinks in clear, simple English, staking out his position like a bear on a kill and daring people to dispute his ground—not a task for the faint of heart. I don't think he would have made it in the United States Department of State.

The hell of it is, Charley is right most of the time. He has a way of cutting through all the nonsense that is elfishly devastating. I remember listening to him on my car radio on the way home from work one dismal afternoon to hear Eckman's Law: "An expert is somebody from out of town." Now, there is a nasty aphorism, and one which, if understood by more people, would put an end to high-priced consultants and save society a lot of money. Why do we assume—in that case it was about getting a new stadium for Baltimore—that somebody from outside one's home town knows the needs of the town more than the people who live there? Or, as Hans Christian Andersen put it, the emperor should dress more warmly.

Charley has been there and done that in more places and in more ways than most sports fans dare to dream about. He really knows this stuff, and in the way of a knowledgeable fan, he says what's true without trying to hide the facts with smoke and mirrors. In this book you'll see how professional basketball really began in America, and more importantly, the difference between what we read in the papers (or, now, see on TV) about sporting events and personalities, and what reality really is. In an area of human enterprise where reality has long since been overtaken by high-flown rhetoric pontificated out by people who've never played the game or coached a game, Charley's oral history of American sports is rather like a cold shower after a hot afternoon.

And that's why I recommend it.

—*Tom Clancy*

Special Eckman Family
Acknowledgment
for Fred Neil

Dad always had a great memory for names and events. He could instantly recall specifics and sporting events from 20, 30, even 40 years past. The family tried for years to get Dad to write this book. In 1994, after two operations for cancer, he finally asked Fred Neil to help him document his thoughts. I believe he knew his remaining time was limited. Many nights Fred would visit Dad's home and be typing away with a big grin as Dad was gesturing and laughing about some memory.

In the early months, Dad had a great time recalling his life's stories to Fred. However, in November 1994 the major medical problems began. He found it increasingly difficult to relate the stories with much enthusiasm. He had accepted reality and realized the life he loved so much was slipping away. Fred recognized the "autobiography" could not be completed and began collecting old memorabilia and stories from the family archives and others who knew about Dad and his career. The roles seem to have been reversed, Fred would visit and entertain Dad about the articles he had found or Eckman stories provided by others. The love and respect between the two old friends touched everyone involved. On many occasions after Fred had left, Dad would lay for hours telling us about the good old times.

What would Dad say to thank Fred for assembling this history? Hearing his voice in each story, I know Dad would say: "Fred, 'It's a very simple game.' ... Thank you, Dear Friend."

Linda Eckman Watts
Daughter

Chapter

1

The Quintessential
Charles Markwood Eckman

Eckman: "Let me tell you why I thought I could coach. I am working the game in Rochester one night between the Rochester Royals and the Minneapolis Lakers at Edgerton Park Arena . . . the place held about 4500 people. The Royals are behind by one point with about 20 seconds to play on the clock and a time out is called. Rochester has the ball. They have to win this game. Lester Harrison was the owner, the coach, the general manager and he sold tickets, too. I'm listening to the huddle to see who's goin'a get the ball. Lester asks, 'What are we going to do?' Well, Bobby Davies asks to get the ball 'cause he can drive on the basket. 'OK,' says Lester, 'Give the ball to Bobby." Bobby "Hooks" Wanzer says, 'Give me the ball, Lester. I've got my shot down.' He had a great set shot. Lester says, 'That's a good idea. Give the ball to 'Hooks.' Now, Arnie Risen, their big Center, says, 'They're laying off me. They ain't coming up on me. Give me the ball.' Lester says, 'That's a good idea. Throw that ball to Risen.' Jack Coleman is sitting there. He says, 'Lester, nobody is coming up on me. I've hit that set shot all night.' Lester says, 'That's a good idea. Throw the ball to Coleman.'

"Four guys are supposed to get this ball. We got 20 seconds to go. I'm saying to myself, 'It's going to be one hell of a play.' I blow the whistle to start play. Now, the only guy that ain't said nothing is Artie Johnson, a big Swede. He was in physical

*training with me during the service. He is sitting in there and
he ain't said nothing. The next thing you know Johnson gets
the ball and puts it in for two and the Rochester Royals beat
the Lakers. The place goes nuts.*

*"As I'm walking off the floor, a writer for the Rochester
newspaper, George Beahon, comes up to Lester Harrison and
says, 'How did you devise that play?' Then, Lester told him how
he devised that play and I knew right then and there that
coaching was for me—a professional liars game."*

—*Charles Markwood Eckman, Jr., Basketball Referee*

Welcome to a celebration of Charley Eckman. Had Charley Eckman been born in New York, Los Angeles or Chicago, he probably would have been widely acclaimed as a sports renaissance man. The fact is, Charley was a sportsman for all seasons. For seven decades he was part of the sports landscape. He may very well have been the best, most colorful basketball referee ever. He was a winning professional basketball coach. In baseball, he was a bat boy, professional player, umpire and baseball scout. In thoroughbred racing, he was a renowned devotee and a heck of a lot more. In broadcasting, he was a huge hit!

In New York, Damon Runyon would have made him a famous horse player. The career of Howard Cosell would have been overshadowed by Eckman. Eckman's name would have been mentioned in the same breath as the great basketball coaches of the era such as Adolph Rupp, Joe Lapchick and Clair Bee . . . and had the cards fallen right, he would have been a highly acclaimed baseball scout for signing a Hall of Famer to a major league baseball contract.

The Basketball Referee

There are legends in the ranks of umpires and referees, but how many of them can you name? The officials are the support players amongst the great celebrities and egos of the games—with perhaps one exception. Long time basketball referee and frequent Eckman partner Hal Grossman said Charley was by far the most popular official in the game, bar none. "I was trailing 15 feet behind him when we had this game at Duke. It was Duke against North Carolina. Now Duke is noted for their hostile student body at the basketball games. When Eckman walked on to the court, the entire Duke student body stood up and gave him an ovation. I never saw it before and I never saw it again," said

(Photo courtesy of Sports Illustrated.*)*

Grossman. He added, "Carolina Coach Dean Smith sees what's going on and his face registers concern. Eckman goes over to Smith and he says 'Don't worry, Dean. I brought Grossman for you.'"

Smith recalls an Atlantic Coast Conference (ACC) pre-season press conference, in 1962 or '63, with all of the ACC basketball coaches and the sports writers covering conference basketball. Smith reports that "Bones" McKinney, the Wake Forest Coach, was asked by a writer if he, "Bones", could have *any* player that could help his team the most, who would he pick? Without hesitating, McKinney said, "Eckman!"

One of America's great sports writers, Frank Deford, certified Eckman's uniqueness in the 1976 *Sports Illustrated* article entitled "Nobody Loves the Ruling Class." Deford wrote, "Whether they're called umpires, referees or judges, those who must decide if it was fair, foul, in, out, over or short are, officially speaking, unappreciated." The exception, Deford noted, was Charley Eckman.

"Of all officials, basketball referees are virtually the only ones who have become personalities. Football referees are all but anonymous, and while a boxing referee like Ruby Goldstein or a baseball umpire like Bill

17

Klem may become recognized as a name, he rarely becomes established as an individual. Who is the most famous baseball umpire today? Ron Luciano? Probably. Not one fan in a thousand would know who Luciano was if he sat down next to him at a coffee counter. By contrast, any basketball fan would not only recognize Richie Powers or John Vanak or Jake O'Donnell, but would also have a fair knowledge of what the man was like personally from having seen him work on the court. Kids used to do imitations of Mendy Rudolph wiping his brow as surely as they did a Dr. J or an Earl the Pearl.

"Rudolph (whose teacher was Charley Eckman) came into prominence at a time when pro basketball had gained a national platform, but colorful characters like Pat Kennedy and Sid Borgia were celebrities long before Mendy ever drew a number in the air. And without doubt no referee anywhere has ever been so well received on and off the court as Charley Eckman. While it seems impossible to attach the word to such a coarse rascal as Eckman, the fact is that he is the one referee in all the world who has become darn near beloved."

"Eckman's Broadway" is the term Don Newbery, one time New York University coach (NYU), described the Mecca of college basketball, Madison Square Garden in New York City.

Newbery's jaw dropped the first time Eckman's name was announced. Game referees were announced after the team players and coaches. Each official had been booed, but the crowd cheered when Charley's name was broadcast over the loud speakers. According to Don, what made the cheering even more unbelievable was the nature of the Garden patrons—hard core street gamblers, fanatic basketball fans, and moneyed, high society types. Newbery said that every one of them were vociferous critics. They cheered and hollered at every Eckman whistle.

Newbery said that Charley would whistle a foul and would invariably put his arm around the offending player and tell him what happened and how to avoid the foul again. Voices from the crowd could be heard shouting "Atta Boy, Charley!," or " You tell 'em, Charley!"

Newbery said that Eckman had those tough, super critical New Yorkers eating out of his hand.

You're the Top

Eckman was consistently rated as one of the top officials in the NBA, the Atlantic Coast Conference and other conferences, if not the best referee. Among his students were two officials who were considered the best in their era, pro ref Mendy Rudolph and Lenny Wirtz from the college ranks.

United Press International wire story, vintage 1967: "Lennie Wirtz, of Cincinnati, Ohio, one of the men working the ACC tournament with Eckman, calls him 'one of the two best I ever saw.' Wirtz says Eckman helps 'younger guys like me learn how to do things right.'"

Hal Grossman became a top rated official in the Atlantic Coast Conference (ACC) and the Eastern Collegiate Athletic Conference (ECAC), "Choo Choo (Eckman) was the only official to take the time to teach me. We would talk for hours. Not many people could have a tutor like Eckman, he taught me more about the game itself, not about the rules of the game . . . he taught me how to handle the game, to control the game, and that's the most important thing for a referee. He taught me the inside, how the officials think, what officials to trust, what teams, and what coaches to worry about." Referee partners nicknamed Charley "Choo Choo" because Charley loved to ride the trains.

James H. Weaver, Atlantic Coast Conference Commissioner, acknowledged Charley's premature retirement and excellence in a letter:

"Dear Charlie: It was with regret that I learned of your resignation as a basketball official from the Atlantic Coast Conference . . . Your work was outstanding and I never worried about the game as long as I knew you were officiating . . . "

Vanderbilt Coach Ray Skinner said, "Eckman is one of the top basketball referees in the United States. He is colorful to a degree. He is perfectly impartial and he keeps the game under control without unnecessary stoppages."

Eckman as a Winning Coach: It's a Very Simple Game

Here is the Eckman philosophy of coaching as reported by Stan Frank in the *Saturday Evening Post:* "Charley Eckman, a referee with no basketball coaching experience whatsoever, became coach of the Ft. Wayne Pistons—and forthwith hauled an also-ran to the top of the league. What's more, he claims it was easy. 'What can you teach All-Americans?' he says, 'How to comb their hair?' . . .

"Thirty-three year old Eckman, the youngest and smallest coach in the league, barely made his high school basketball team in Baltimore. 'I had two handicaps,' he says, 'No height or talent.'"

1955-56. Fort Wayne wins Western Division Championship. Mel Hutchins, who made the winning basket, being congratulated by (L to R): George Yardley, Corky Devlin, Chuck Noble, Odie Spears, Bobby Houbregs, Chuck Cooper, and Frankie Brian.

Then there was Eckman the coaching genius, as reported by Wilton Garrison, Sports Editor of the *Charlotte Observer*, when Charley was lecturing at a coaching clinic after winning the NBA (Western Division) championship. Also on the program were Clair Bee of Long Island, Eddie Hickey of St. Louis and Adolph Rupp, of Kentucky.

" 'Bee, who had written several books on basketball and was a noted lecturer, came out wearing a cap lettered LIU,' recalled Charlie. 'For two hours he talked . . .

" 'Hickey walked out wearing a shirt bearing a St. Louis emblem. He also talked for two hours . . . Rupp wore both a cap and shirt with Kentucky in big letters on them. He talked for two hours . . . when he finished everybody was limp from blocking shots at the basket.

"Last came Eckman. 'I didn't have either a sweat shirt or cap, for Fort Wayne didn't have that much money. I walked up to the blackboard, eyed the tired group and told them: Gentlemen, in my coaching I try to get the five biggest, fastest and best-shooting boys I can find.

" 'Then the three big men run, toward the basket and the two little guards either pass the ball or dribble it past mid-court, toss it to one of the big men, who turns and shoots. Then I jump off the bench and yell: 'Defense! Defense! Get back down here d---- quick!' That, my friends, is what I do in my coaching.'

" 'That night all three of them visited my room and give me a lecture on conducting coaching clinics. 'What are you trying to do,' screamed Rupp, 'break up one of our best rackets? Take hours to talk and after you get them confused you've got it made . . . .' "

What are the possibilities of a basketball referee officiating in an NBA basketball game and then coaching a team in the All-Star game? Charley Eckman, sometimes called Cholly by his friends, did it. Eckman officiated in the first NBA All-Star game, coached in two, and was the winning coach of an underdog West team in one game. Obviously, no one can ever do that again.

> Eckman: "The East had Dolph Schayes, Harry Gallatin, and Paul Arizin. These fellows could shoot and rebound. I put in my four big men . . . Mel Hutchins, Larry Foust, George Yardley, and Jack Coleman. I only had three Guards for the All Star game and I used Guard Slater Martin with my four big guys. Now, Hutchins could guard a little man as well as a big man. He

1954 NBA West All-Star Team. Back row (L to R): Jack Coleman, Vern Mikkelsen, Arnie Risen, Larry Foust, Bob Pettit, Jim Pollard. Front row: Charley, Andy Phillip, Bobby Wanzer, Slater Martin, Frank Selvy, George Yardley.

was a great defensive player. I can't emphasize that enough.

"My big guys could rebound and we killed them on the boards. Martin couldn't see too well to shoot from the outside, but he passed the ball. He would throw it up there somewhere and we would go get it. George Senesky, coach of the Philadelphia Warriors who beat me in the playoffs in my second year with the Pistons, stayed with a pat lineup. He used the two Guards and two Forwards and a Center.

"I would get in a huddle and I would tell my team, 'Crash the boards . . . hit the boards . . . I don't give a damn what happens, hit those boards. Hutchins walked away with those rebounds. Yardley was jumpin' out of the arena and we beat them on the boards. While they were standing around, we were beating their brains out and we wound up beating the East by eight points. The smart guys said we couldn't win if the East used only three players!"

His success with his big men who could play and guard Guards opened a new avenue of thought in basketball circles.

Newspaper Headlines from the Past

● *St. Louis Post Dispatch*: **"St. Louis Ace Voted Top Player; Coach's Strategy Praised"**

● *United Press*: **"Eckman Wows 'Em Again"** by Norman Millet

● *Winston-Salem Journal*: **"Charley Eckman: Players Referee, He's Jolly . . . Jaunty . . . Tough . . . and Respected"** by Bob Cole

● *Durham Morning Herald*: **"Eckman Leads Tourney Referees"** by Jack Horner ". . . Charley Eckman our favorite referee and possibly the best in the country . . ."

● *Berk's County Newspaper*: **"Eckman Tells "Em How at 21st Annual Banquet of Berk's County Basketball Officials"**

● *Local Newspaper*: **"Eckman Wows 'Em at Hitchcock Awards"**

● *Washington Post*: **"Basketball's Sad Day—Eckman Retires"** by William Gildea

Eckman at the Races: Damon, Are You Listening?

Runyon would have loved Eckman. Who else but Eckman would have a Catholic priest on his knees praying for a horse to win for a Protestant and Jewish ticket holder who happened to be the owner of the track.

Eckman: "I bring Father Neil O'Donnell, who I got to know from St. Agnes Hospital, to Laurel Race Track. The track owner, John Shapiro, a multi-millionaire who pioneered international thoroughbred competition in the United States with the **Laurel International Race**, invites us up to his Board Room. This is a beautiful place to watch the races because its completely enclosed with a great view of the finish line.

"Now, John and I are going down fast. We're in the hole. Father Neil ain't bettin,' but he's enjoying watching the action. Finally, Shapiro says to me, 'Its time to stop losing. We got to have a winner here.' We bet sixty-five dollars on a horse with four to one odds.

Charley searches for a winner.

"The horse race starts and down the final turn they come and our horse is starting to move from the back of the pack. Shapiro and I are rompin' and stompin' and hollerin'. Shapiro don't need the money but he wanted a winner.

"I said, 'Father Neil, do something!' With that he said, 'Charles, I will.' I turned around and watched the horses coming down the stretch. Father Neil says, 'How's this for openers!' I turn around and see that Father Neil is on his knees praying. Johnny Shapiro got to laughing so hard his contact lens fell out of his eye.

"It worked. Our horse won and paid $8.80 for a two dollar bet and we had $65.00 to win on him. Here was the priest, a class guy, and he is helping out a Jew and Protestant by praying. It was better than the movies."

Eckman and Baseball—A Hollywood Star?

Major Art Reichle, who had been the baseball coach at UCLA before World War II, had a very close up view of PFC Eckman at the Yuma Army Air Force Base.

"Dear Chuck . . . Spoke to Oscar Reichow this P.M. and have arranged a try-out for you with the Hollywood Stars. The only hitch being that you must report immediately if not sooner to the Hollywood Ball Park at Fairfax and Beverly Boulevard . . . Gave you a good build up and told Oscar that you were the best hitter I ever saw. (That is for hitting behind the runner).

Seriously, I do hope you can come out immediately for I think that if you are in as good condition as you said you should be able to play on the Coast this season . . ."

Eckman as a Sportcaster

As a sportscaster, like Howard Cosell, there was no middle ground on Eckman. With both, you liked them or you turned them off. Public reaction to Eckman's sportscasts was parallel to Cosell's on a local level. But Cosell had no concept of what it was like to be inside the world of sports, in the trenches, on the playing field, on the court or any other metaphor for playing the game. Eckman was there . . . and if he could hit the high hard one, he would have excelled in baseball as he excelled in everything else he did.

Another edge Eckman had over Cosell is that Charley was funnier. Eckman: "I went to Eli Hanover's son's brisk (sic) at Sinai Hospital today. That's the first time I've seen a clipping without a 15 yard penalty!" Hanover was a fight promoter in Baltimore.

The Birth of a Book: A Personal Perspective

In July of 1994, I received a telephone call. The distinctive voice on the other end said, "Freddy Neil! Its time to get goin' on the book!" Since graduating from college, only my late parents and my Godparents called me Freddy, except my daughter's Godfather, Charley Eckman. Charley was ready to chronicle the adventures that made him the larger than life figure he was.

To me, Charles Markwood Eckman, Jr. was an extraordinary entertainer, a Danny Kaye or Robin Williams of the sports world. Charley's mind was inventive . . . comically inventive. He was a brilliant ad libber, although he could read a script and make it sound "Eckmanese."

On the basketball court, his spontaneous humor added to the proceedings and did not detract from the game. Joe Lapchick, one of the outstanding coaches in college and pro ball of his era, said of Eckman, "When Charley Eckman works, you can sit on the bench and know the best job is being done. Eckman has a rare quality, a feeling of communication with everyone involved. You have confidence in him at all times."

Charley, as the anecdotes in this book, from him and about him, will reveal, was the master of the quip and in control of whatever endeavor he was involved in and not just in basketball. On radio or television, at the racetrack, or in baseball, Eckman was one of a kind, always funny and always in command, with one exception. Had he a better command of picking the right horses to win at the racetrack, he would have been a multi-millionaire.

A Guide

Categorizing Charley presents a problem. His basketball and broadcasting careers can be illustrated chronologically. But, his involvement in baseball and horse racing span his life from a young kid to 1995. He served as an ad hoc advisor to Peter Angelos, the owner of the Baltimore Orioles. He was the Master of Ceremonies of the Penn National Race track "World Series of Handicapping." It seemed easier to cover his lifetime of activities in horse racing and baseball in chapters of their own.

Eckman, who preferred to spell his first name "Charley" rather than "Charlie" as it appears in a number of quotes throughout the book, was no angel.

The purpose of this book is not to reveal warts, however, but to preserve those words and things that enriched the lives of those millions of people who saw or heard or who knew Charley Eckman,—one of a kind, a piece of Americana, who added to sports history with his achievements, and who painted our world with rich, vibrant colors of laughter in the process. It is a celebration of the life and times of Charley Eckman.

Eckman, a master of the court and the quip. How did he get that way? Here is a look at this remarkable man.

Chapter

2

Eckman Unbridled

*Like Norman Rockwell creating a painting, the confident and col-
orful Eckman steered ten guys up and down a hardwood floor, letting
them think they were the main attraction, but all the while stealing a
small hunk of the show for himself. After all, with one glance, you
knew who painted a Rockwell.*

*It wasn't that Eckman set out to do this. It was just his way, his
demeanor. He had a style all his own, like Rockwell. Charley was so
quick, loud and dominant, he could have governed play without a
whistle if the rules called for it.*

"Charley is Charley," *Baltimore Sun* sports writer Cameron Snyder once wrote, "and nobody is going to change him." Not that anybody
wanted to because nobody ever officiated a game the way Eckman did,
and it's likely nobody ever will. He's the kind of guy who makes a good
game better, certainly funnier.

From the hoopla of the day emerged this diminutive, slightly bowlegged, square-jawed, stripe-shirted guy who revolutionized the game
with antics that set the crowd on its ear. First a whistle, then a wiggle
here, a kick there, this Lilliputian among giants, ball balanced on his
hip, scurries to the point of contact and nails the culprit with a defini-
tive, "Youuu!" If you didn't think you fouled anybody, you were gestured
and talked into it by the time Charley got through. Oh sure, he made
mistakes, but he never made excuses. There weren't many mistakes

though, and that's what won Charley respect in every league he ever officiated in.

    Eckman's observations on fans: "Fans complain to me that it costs so much to go to the ballpark and take their kids . . . the tickets, the parking, the food . . . but tell them that they can't go, they'll jump over a line of alligators to get to the front gate."

    Eckman's observations on a womanizing ball player: "He gets more ass than all the toilet seats in East Baltimore."

    Eckman's observations on life: "An expert is a guy from out-of-town."

Eckman and How He Got That Way

    Charles Markwood Eckman, Jr. was born street smart in 1921 in Southeast Baltimore and was raised in Northeast Baltimore, at Hoffman Street and Luzerne Ave. He attended #85 Elementary School and Clifton Park Junior High. As a kid, his family bounced from one neighborhood to another. His father, Charles Markwood Eckman, Sr., worked as a meat cutter in a grocery store until he entered the Army to fight in that war to end all wars, World War I.

12-year-old Charley, shortly after his father's death.

The senior Eckman had been gassed during the allied Meuse-Argonne offensive in France. Charley did not get to know his father well. A few trips to see baseball games helped to wet young Charley's appetite for sports. His dad was hospitalized frequently because of his wounds and died in 1933. His death, during the great depression when Charley was 12 years old, left his wife, Marie Margaret, to fend for Charley and herself.

Eckman: "My mother was getting $40.00 a month pension from my father's World War I service. We lived in a $16.00 a month apartment on North Avenue after moving from Hoffman street. We started playing musical chairs with the apartments on North Avenue. We would get an apartment and we would last a few months and then we would have to move. It's a very simple game. We didn't have any money."

Several incidents help illuminate Charley's early life. One of the apartments he and mother lived in was near the Bond Bakery, a commercial baking company. The aroma of that baking bread waifting through the late night air was a siren song to the young, hungry Charley. He sneaked out of the apartment, rounded up a couple of buddies, and they launched a sneak attack through an open window on the loaves of bread. He fashioned a spear, of sorts, with a rope and a knife. The trio liberated several loaves of bread from the conveyor belt.

Suddenly, a voice rang out, "What are you kids doin'." It was a guy from the bakery. Charley told him that were hungry. The bakery guy said, "Well, at least you're honest and he gave them several more loaves of bread. The man then added a bonus. He took all three kids to a Boy Scout meeting the next week to keep the boys from further mischief.

Eckman: "I walked into that meeting and see all these guys dressed up in these scout uniforms making knots. The bakery guy said we can join the scouts and get the uniforms for only $10.95. I couldn't come up with 10 cents much less $10.95. I mean, he could have asked for a $1,000,000. Besides, if I had tried to tie them knots, I probably would have hung myself."

At the age of 12, Charley did find employment and developed a friendship with Joe Cambria, who exposed the young Eckman to an insider's view of professional baseball. Charley went to work at Cam-

All-Maryland Second Baseman Eckman, 1939-40, in Baltimore City College uniform.

bria's Bugle Coat and Apron Company as a helper on a delivery truck. Charley said he had a thousand pimples on this face and felt like a millionaire because he made $7.00 a week.

Charley played a lot of amateur baseball growing up, as a first or second baseman. He had a flare that made him an All Star and later earned him a pro baseball contract. In 1941, Charley received a letter from James Enright, Chairman, All Star Committee.

"This is to inform you that you have been accorded the honor of playing on the All Star Team of the Maryland Amateur Baseball Association on August 29th at 6:30 P.M. at Oriole Park. The program for the evening calls for our All Star Team to play the Orioles at 6:30 P.M. following which the Orioles will play Newark of the International League. I would appreciate it if you would make every effort to be present at Oriole Park not later than 5:30 P. M. Friday, August 29th . . . ." Charley was also an All Maryland Second Baseman on the City College high school team.

But Charley had his sights on "being somebody" and he didn't think that baseball would get him there. He used his street smarts to get into refereeing.

While he was attending Baltimore City College, one of two all male public high schools in Baltimore, the refereeing bug bit. Many City College alumni went on to distinguish themselves in the fields of medicine, law, education, broadcasting and sports. Actor Edward Everett Horton, TV great Gary Moore, and Yankee pitcher Tommy Byrne attended City College. Two term Governor of Maryland, William Donald Schaefer, was Charley's classmate.

Eckman: "I started refereeing basketball at the age of 16, because I needed the money. It's as simple as that. I watched Jim Boyer and other referees work around town, including Johnny Neun . . . he used to be with the Yankees . . . scout/manager/first baseman. I knew I would get $2.00 a game and that meant a lot to me.

"I knew I could referee. I knew I wasn't going to make it as a basketball player. I wasn't going to the top in the baseball park . . . couldn't hit . . . didn't have the power. I was a skinny kid but I was a better baseball man than a basketball player. Being a referee was the quickest way to the top."

Charley approached Boyer, who made his mark as an American League baseball umpire, after Boyer had refereed a high school basketball game. Boyer encouraged Eckman, and Charley was off and running . . . literally.

Charley at age 21.

Eckman claims he could run all night and he ran to three different games on Sundays at three different locations all over Baltimore to collect $2.00 a game. After the last game he would walk home because no streetcars or buses were running.

Charley saved money by walking and made money by officiating at as many games as he could. At first, his mother was suspicious as to where the money came from. Eckman: "I'll never forget my mother's bewildered look when I dumped $38.00 in her lap one day. 'Why this is more than your father ever made in the grocery store,' she said."

Eckman officiated in Baltimore until he was called into the Army Air Corp in 1941. He reached the "big time" by refereeing in the Baltimore Basketball League, where he got $7.50 a game. . . . and did he put on a show for the "big bucks".

Eckman: "I was a one man show . . . sure, I was a showman! I knew I was a showman and I did it. I put on a show because I wanted to be somebody. I attracted attention. How the hell else would you get to the top?

"I did the showman stuff naturally . . . but if I saw you hack a man, I reenacted the scene . . . and I could jump, and I could run and I had a big voice. I could stop a freight train going through the tunnel with that voice. When I hollered 'Blue,' meaning the team wearing the blue uniforms, everybody and his brother knew it."

Before he answered the call of his country, Eckman played professional baseball and got married.

Chapter

3

Eckman Bridled

Baseball Hall of Famer Hoyt Wilhelm and Charley Eckman were teammates in Class D Ball in Mooresville, North Carolina. In those days the minor league teams, with a few exceptions, were independently owned. Eckman, with his fielding skills and fiery leadership, was signed to play with the Mooresville Moores. Wilhelm, the greatest knuckle ball pitcher of all time, who lived in Cornelius, North Carolina, about eight miles from Mooresville, became a member of the team.

Eckman: "So, down I go to Mooresville, North Carolina in 1940. Hoyt Wilhelm, the Hall of Famer, is trying out for my team. Our manager was a fellow named Johnny Hicks who was also the team catcher. He had a fit trying to catch Hoyt's knuckler. Hoyt would throw it and Hicks would try to catch the ball on his knees . . . he would try to bang the ball down in the dirt . . . he had to chase the ball to the backstop when it got away from him . . . which happened often.

"Now, when the batter would get two strikes, Hicks didn't want to be embarrassed by missing the ball. So, he would call for a fast ball or a curve. At that time, Wilhelm didn't have a good fast ball or a curve. Pretty soon everybody in the league knew that if Hoyt got two strikes on the batter . . . here comes a hittable pitch . . . then, Bingo! . . . let the good times roll. That's why Wilhelm stayed five years down in Mooresville."

Wilhelm didn't get sent to a higher league until Paul Florence, the catcher and scout for the Cincinnati Reds, saw Wilhelm pitch. He signed him to go to the Birmingham, Alabama team after buying his contract from Mooresville.

A Diamond in the Rough

As a baseball player, Charley admits that he not only couldn't hit the "high, hard one" but he couldn't hit the "low soft ones." He earned $85.00 a month playing in North Carolina. The now defunct North Carolina State League was considered a good Class D league at the time.

The only farm team in the North Carolina State League in 1940 prior to World War II was Coolemaee, North Carolina, in the St. Louis Cardinal Farm system. The Cardinals were known to be cheap. Eckman was getting $85.00 a month while the best player over at Coolemaee was getting $75.00 a month.

15-year-old Charley (far right) on 1937 Baltimore Junior League Championship Team, the Apache Indians. Shown as the team's infield (L to R): Otts Mickimmon, Lou Thoman, Johnny Gehrman, Teddy Foster, and Charley.

And Still Going Strong

Eckman's career as a professional baseball player was short lived (damned high hard one). As an 18-year-old infielder, he nearly got traded from the Moores because the Goldsboro team manager/third baseman Mack Arnett liked his style.

Eckman: "The Moores went to spring training in 1940 and we played exhibition games against teams in the Coastal Plain League. We go to play against Goldsboro. Mack was tall and skinny and a very nice guy.

"I had a pretty good day. I get a couple of hits but we are losing two to nothing in the eighth inning. I'm on third base and I have a wild desire to show off. I'm a kid, a mere rookie. I take off and steal home. There is no reason in this world for me to steal home because that one run ain't going to help us.

"Norman Small, who was our best hitter, was at the plate. When he saw me coming, his eyes got big as a baseball. He had to be wonderin' what in the hell is going on here? I slide home and scored but we get beat two to one.

"After the game, our manager, Johnny Hicks, has a meeting with Arnett. Arnett comes over and says to me, he says, 'Kid, would you like to play here?' I said, 'Yes, sir! Mr. Arnett.' Heck, I want to play anywhere . . . and I wasn't sure I was going to make the team in Mooresville. So he says to Hicks, 'I'll give you five hundred dollars for him. I like the kid.' Hicks turned him down.

"In 1994, I am looking at the papers and I see a story on Mack Arnett who is a scout for the Orioles down in Ashville, North Carolina. Mack is now 92 years old and still in baseball scouting, we call it 'Bird Dogging,' for the Orioles.

"Hicks, by the way, became the head of Burlington Mills. When he died he left a fortune to his alma mater, Wake Forest."

Eckman did eventually get traded to the Newton-Conover Twins. The local newspaper carried a report on the Twins win over the Hickory Rebels. "A new shortstop, Charlie Eckman, former Mooresville player is now working with the Twins . . . He covered the hot spot in fine fashion and brought applause from the fans with a throw, made from the sitting position."

Eckman, the Romantic

After the season was over, Charley stayed in town long enough to meet his wife of 53 years, the former Wilma Howard. They were married in November of 1941.

> Eckman: "She was a waitress in a restaurant. I gave her a quarter tip on Tuesday. On Wednesday, we dated . . . Thursday, we didn't . . . Friday, I said let's get married and she said 'Let's go!' For $5.00, we got married in York, South Carolina, by a Justice of the Peace.
>
> "Very simple game . . . make them decisions . . . make those snap decisions they last longer, that way you don't have time to worry about it. And as a result, we grew up together during our 53 years of married life. We are still in there, still learning, still getting along . . . it's a tough league, but by the same token we made it.
>
> "I borrowed $5.00 from her, put it down on a ring, got the ring . . . I paid for all this stuff later . . . I only had $8.00 left. We got on the train in Charlotte, North Carolina with the $10.00 I borrowed from the bootlegger in Mooresville."

Wilma's version of the courtship goes like this. She said that she was busy at the time her boss at the restaurant asked her to serve dessert to a customer, a chocolate sundae. He introduced himself at the cash register and asked her out. Three days later they went across the state line and got married. Then, the couple boarded the day coach for Baltimore.

The newlyweds moved into the apartment with Charley's mother. The two Mrs. Eckmans agreed to disagree on most everything. It was rough on Wilma, a small town North Carolina gal in a big city. Her mother-in-law did not take kindly to losing her only child. Eventually, the couple moved in with Charley's grandfather at 223 Stricker Street where number one son, Charles Barry, now age 53, was born. When Charley went into the Army Air Corps. Wilma moved back to Mooresville, where the first of their three daughters, Linda Lou, was born.

While Eckman was back in Baltimore awaiting his call up to the Air Corps, he officiated in basketball games and picked up a couple of bucks by playing for some good semi-pro baseball teams . . . the Brooklyn AA's, Mt. Washington, and then Bethlehem Steel to play ball and to work at

Christmas 1955 in Fort Wayne. L to R: Janet, Charley, Gail holding family dog "Happy," Barry, Wilma (wife), and Linda. (Photo courtesy of Fort Wayne Sentinel.*)*

the coke ovens for $29.00 a week. Bill Lombardi, at Westinghouse, coaxed Charley over there for a job that paid $32.00 a week. With Charley on board, Westinghouse won the Industrial League championship.

In those days, industrial plants around Baltimore gearing up for the war effort hired ball players. Charley stayed with Westinghouse until he enlisted and was later called up for duty.

As a referee, he handled the top club games in Baltimore. The teams had names like the Stonewalls, the Arundel Boat Club, the YMHA, the Susquehannocks, and the Lithuanian Americans.

One day, Eckman got a call from Father Kelly, of Fourteen Holy Martyrs, who asked him to come down to take a look at the sign he just put up advertising a game. Eckman recalls: "He had a sign out on Pratt Street, 'Flatheads vs the Heebs. Come Early. Wednesday night.' Now, that meant the Lithuanian Americans were playing the Young Men's Hebrew Association. We packed Fourteen Holy Martyrs gym that night. And that was quite a crowd, maybe eight hundred people. Today, that sign would most likely get you ten years in jail!"

Finally, not only did Lucky Strike Green go to war, but so did Eckman.

Chapter
4

Darn Tootin'

In the February 19, 1955 edition of the Saturday Evening Post *article by Stanley Frank, one of Charley's travails on the court was chronicled. Wrote Frank, "Then there was a delicate contretemps at El Centro, California after the war, when ex-Corporal Eckman needed ready money to support his wife and three children. He went on tour as a referee with the All-American Redheads, a girls' team that played any bunch of men foolish enough to venture into the arena with them. The Redhead center was a a six foot, six-inch misanthrope who committed frightful indignities on male opponents, taking outrageous advantage of the maxim that a gent never slugs a lady in public regardless of the provocation.*

"That dame had a build that would make a skinny boy look like Marilyn Monroe," Eckman says reflectively, "but with her bony elbows and knees she cut guys to ribbons. What a beast!"

After watching the hachet woman in a couple of games, Eckman felt he would lose his union card in humanity if he did not curb her atrocities. He finally called a foul on her when she ran into a man so violently that he was struck in the face with a pass and suffered a broken nose.

"What's the foul for?" she screeched.

"You can't bump into a player and use you . . . your chest that way," Eckman retorted.

The Redhead was a real pro. Her competitive drive was stronger than her vanity. "Where do you see a chest?" she demanded.

"I'm giving you the benefit of the doubt," Eckman snapped.

The young lady patted Eckman on the head when the fans within earshot stopped whooping hysterically. "That's a GREAT GAG, Kid," she said. "We'll have to use it tomorrow night."

That incident occurred shortly after Eckman was mustered out of the Army, but before that . . .

This is the Air Corp, PFC Eckman

Charley was finally called to duty in the Army Air Corp. From the Induction Center in Greensboro, North Carolina, he was sent to Western Reserve University to train as a Bombardier.

Eckman: "I flunked out of Bombardier school after the plane I was flying in, a Piper Cub type trainer, cracked up. The damn thing caught fire over Lake Erie near Cleveland. The pilot told me to get out. I said 'no way I'm leaving.' He said 'you'll be court marshalled.' I said, 'I just left.' So, I bailed out of that thing and landed by the railroad tracks . . . and that scared the hell out of

U.S. Army Air Force Bombardier School, Cleveland, Ohio, 1942.

1944 Yuma Army Air Force base. Capt. Clem Swaggerty (L) with Charley.

me. I messed with the toilet for three weeks after that . . . So now we leave Cleveland, they ship me out to Yuma to attend gunnery school at the Yuma Air Force Base. I said to myself, 'Ain't this a beautiful place. I mean . . . lotsa' sand . . . sand fleas . . . and scorpions' . . . they were all down there having lunch. I would look at them babies and I said man! This is the place for me."

While Charley was doing physical education training, he overheard a Sergeant telling another guy that they did not have an umpire at his softball game last night. Eckman told the Sergeant he had experience and he volunteered to handle the game that night. He did so with his usual flair and suddenly his services were in great demand . . . all over the Western U. S. of A..

Eckman: "Colonel Phillips comes to see me and says, 'Do you do this all the time?' I said, 'Sure.' Captain Clem Swaggerty, who was a star football player at the College of the Pacific, chimes in. He said, 'That's the best game we have ever had around here. Where are you stationed?' I said, 'In the barracks over there in the sand. Hell, there were barracks in the sand everywhere.' He tells this Staff Sergeant to bring me over to him the next morning."

Eckman received an offer he couldn't refuse long before that line was made famous in a certain movie. The Captain asked him if he wanted to stay at the Yuma Air Base. Charley became a physical training instructor for wounded servicemen and after hours he officiated volleyball and basketball games, umpired softball, and played for the post baseball team. Major Art Reichle, who had been the baseball coach at the University of California in Los Angeles, named Charley captain of the team.

Army Air Force Sports League Bulletin (AAFWFTC) No. 12 dated 5 Oct. 45: "Yuma AAF, Pacific Coast Service Champion–1945: Yuma AAF won the Pacific Coast Service Softball title, Wednesday, 3 Oct 45, at Fresno, Calif., by defeating Hammer Field, champions of 4th Air Force and Bay Area Service competition in a 1–0 shut-out before a capacity crowd.

". . . With the reduction of training and transfer of key physical training personnel from Yuma, PFC Chuck Eckman took over the reigns as playing manager and coach. Yuma, previously considered a backwoods rookie aggregation, in beating Hammer Field, last year's National champions, has proven the value of an extensive inter-post softball competitve program."

Yuma was the Air Force base of the stars. Among those passing through were Charley Trippi, the football star, Grady Hatton, the Major League baseball player . . . and Ronald Reagan, then a Second Lieutenant. Reagan and Gene Raymond, another movie star, who was married to Jeanette McDonald, the singer and movie actress, played volleyball, with Eckman officiating. Even Bob Hope visited but didn't perform there.

With the start of the basketball season, Eckman's services were in greater demand. His style of officiating was a sensation and his colonel, one "Snuffy" Smith, received requests from throughout the Western Army Air Force Command: "We have a game and we want Eckman!!" Gene Raymond frequently piloted the plane that took Eckman places far and wide in the West.

Luke Field against Williams Field, games in Phoenix with the Webbcos, owned by New York Yankee owner, Del Webb . . . off to Fresno in a B-26, then down to Los Angeles for a game at the Pan Pacific Center arena. Colonel Smith went along on several trips. He hadn't a clue about basketball until he got an eyeful of Eckman in action.

Eckman: "I flew up and down the West Coast, courtesy of the Air Corp, officiating games. They had pretty good teams over there. They had what they called the American League. I even officiated in that league after the war. I would be going from Yuma all over the West Coast flying, training, flying, training. The Western Command basketball playoff was held in Phoenix, and I had the game. The Colonel was right with me. He learned basketball in a hell of a hurry.

"We'd leave the airbase twice a week maybe. Hop on a B-26 and fly up, fly back. Anyhow, we got along fine. That's the way it was for all my years in the Service. I was umpiring, playing ball, and officiating.

"I sent Wilma $800.00 and I kept $20.00. At night, when I wasn't refereeing or umpiring, I was hustling in pool rooms in Yuma and Winterhaven, California."

U.S. Army Air Force Softball Champs. Player/manager Eckman kneeling third from right.

Gambling was legal in Winterhaven and Charley became the patsy in poker games. It was probably the only time he played "the stiff." The only time he would enter a hand in poker was when he had kings or better.

He got paid $5.00 a night to sit there all night and get people to play, the guys from the Air Corp, the Flyboys, the Captains, and Lieutenants who had money. They wanted to gamble. He'd stay at the hotel and go back to the base in the morning. As a PT instructor he didn't have to tell "nobody nothin'."

Eckman: "If you beat anybody at the end of the night, you'd leave the table. I'd say, I got to go piss or something. The guy running the game would take my money 'cause I'd leave it on the table. I wasn't allowed to take any money with me. All you had was the chips. So you take the chips and shove them over there and say 'Watch these chips for me' and get the hell out."

Charley did his part as a physical training instructor. He worked with the men who had been wounded in the war. He worked on their bodies and he told stories that were good for their souls. Eckman: "I think I made Sergeant the day the war ended, but never got a chance to wear the stripes. They retired me as a Corporal."

The Yuma and Hollywood Whistle Stops

Charley mustered out of the Service but stayed in Yuma. He sent for Wilma and the kids and ensconced them in an apartment while continuing his whistle stopping ventures. Their second daughter, Anita Gail, was born in 1946 and Janet Marie came along back in Baltimore in 1949.

Eckman: "I'd go up and down the West Coast refereeing games between the San Diego Dons, Oakland Bittners, with big Frank Lubin, who played in the 1936 Olympics for the U.S., from 20th Century Fox . . . he had been a pretty good ball player in his day and the Hollywood Shamrocks . . . they were owned by J.P. Carroll, a make-up artist for the Hollywood stars . . . he had a pretty good basketball team.

"I got a reputation out there on the West Coast and they wanted me to stay in Hollywood . . . I was perfect for Hollywood . . . but I didn't know it. I did bit parts in movies. I did twelve Pathe' News newsreels. They would have me come in as a spot player. I think I got $15.00 for the part. I was a spectator, a runner or a holler guy in the crowd. I made that money plus $35.00 a night in the Pan Pacific Center in Los Angeles where I refereed.

"Basketball was not a big thing out there, but this was a stepping stone. I refereed high school ball, college ball. We'd go over there to L.A. on weekends. I'd referee the game on Saturday night in Hollywood."

Eckman also officiated college and semi-pro games in Phoenix for the Southwestern Conference, formerly the Border Conference. That was when the University of Arizona had schools at Mesa, Tempe, and down in Tucson. Rudy Lobeck ran the Tempe team at the University. Charley would go into New Mexico, Abilene, and at Hardin-Simmons.

Making a living for his family required more than refereeing. Charley, on occasion, served as a Deputy Sheriff. He was also a bus dispatcher, and he ran a pool hall.

Eckman: "I ran a pool room, shot nine ball, Snooker. I had a big Indian, one of them Yuma Indians working for me, a big strong guy . . . steady . . . never said nothing . . . just racked the balls. I give him a couple of bucks and a cigar. We had a great relationship."

Deputy Sheriff Eckman, who would later become a Judge of the Orphans Court in Anne Arundel County, Maryland, worked for Sheriff Beard in Yuma. Deputy Charley would ride up to Florence, Arizona with the prisoners from the Yuma jail . . . four at a time.

Eckman: "The sheriff would handcuff all of them, and he gave me a gun. I could have thrown that gun faster than I could have shot it . . . and thrown it better and more accurate. He and I would ride up and he would tell them boys when he would let 'em out at Gila Bend . . . it was a stopping off place where they could drink and go to the toilet . . . he would tell them, 'You know fellows, if you try to get away I'm going to try to kill you and, therefore, my Deputy has the same right.' And I said to myself, ain't this a mess. I'd most likely have to run out there and tackle them. So, off we go and I'd get $15.00 for going to Florence with Sheriff Beard."

By 1947, life in hot Yuma began drying up. The pool room Charley was running fizzled. He sent Wilma and the kids to live with her mother until he got reestablished in Baltimore.

Chapter

5

The Original Red Hot Referee

Eckman: "I was a production clerk, I was in charge of hiding the parts and then finding them. The only way you could get overtime was, if you said, 'This bushing belongs in bin #26.' You would then throw it in bin #12. So then, the other clerks couldn't find it . . . then you go and find it for them . . . and that's how you got overtime. It was a very simple game!"
—Charles Markwood Eckman, Jr., Westinghouse Employee

You can go home again and Charley headed back to Baltimore. He went back to work at the Westinghouse plant located on Wilkens Avenue. Bill Lombardi, who was instrumental in hiring Charley before the War, opened the door for him again. While Eckman played baseball for the Westinghouse team, his official job title was "production clerk."

Charley brought his family back to Baltimore from North Carolina and did what comes naturally . . . he got back into refereeing in the area.

The Basketball Association of America (BAA) had started in 1947. Eckman wrote to the Chief Referee, Pat Kennedy. Kennedy had already received letters recommending Charley from some of the West Coast basketball officials.

Eckman: "Kennedy was the supervisor for the BAA back when basketball was basketball. He was a New Yorker, quite a showman also and a good guy. He hired me and I would referee

(Photo courtesy of Sports Illustrated.*)*

on weekends. I'd go to Providence where Roland Hemond, the Orioles' and former Chicago White Sox General Manager, was like the equipment manager for the Providence Steamrollers. Hank Soar, a major league baseball umpire, who had played football for the New York Giants, was the coach.

"It seemed like every Saturday I was in Providence. The next day I would go to Boston to work the Celtics games. Then, I came home and go to work at Westinghouse on Monday.

"Well, Westinghouse has a strike. I said to myself, 'Ain't this awful. I don't need no strike with a wife and three kids.' I called Maurice Podoloff, who ran the BAA and became the Commissioner of the NBA when it was formed. I said, "Look I'm ready to go full time.' He said, 'I need a Western Referee.' So out I go in 1948. I refereed in Sheboygan . . . Moline . . . Minot . . . Hello, Ford City . . . here comes Denver, there goes St. Louis . . . Minneapolis . . . all good towns. The BAA games were played all over the country those days, not just the home city."

The early days of post World War II professional basketball were very humble. Salaries of players were lousy. For most players and referees, a "real" off season job was a must. In 1948, when Westinghouse workers were on strike, Charley did a short stint as a tax investigator for the State of Maryland Sales Tax Division.

The game grew haltingly. Musical chairs and franchises had a lot in common. The owners of the teams frequently served as coaches and ticket sellers. The arenas, with a few exceptions, were small and primitive by today's standards. Most owners operated on a shoestring and lived from hand to mouth, and any other cliche that denotes an operation near abject poverty.

From those humble beginnings of the NBA, nee BAA, the stable franchises like the New York Knicks and Boston Celtics are alive and well today. The Philadelphia Warriors now live in San Francisco and the Minneapolis Lakers are in Los Angeles. The original Baltimore Bullets folded. A Chicago franchise became the new Baltimore Bullets that now represent Washington and the Pistons moved from Fort Wayne to Detroit. The other teams that have moved or died since 1946 include the Washington Capitols, Toronto Huskies, St. Louis Bombers, Providence Steamrollers, Pittsburgh Ironman, Detroit Falcons, Cleveland Rebels, Chicago Stags, Packers, and Zephers, Rochester Royals, Indianapolis Jets and Olympians, Syracuse Nationals, Tri-Cities Blackhawks, Sheyboygan Redskins, St. Louis Bombers, the original Denver Nuggets, Waterloo Hawks, Milwaukee Hawks (Atlanta), San Diego Rockets, Cincinnati Royals, Buffalo Braves, Kansas City-Omaha Kings (Sacramento), New Orleans Jazz (Utah).

Most teams in the NBA and the league remained on the edge of bankruptcy until the commissioner David Stern came along in 1984 to raise the NBA to its highest heights.

Eckman points out that in the early 1980s, the NBA had at least five teams nearly bankrupt and a large number of its players reportedly on drugs. Given major league baseball's strike in 1994 and the fans reaction to it at the start of the season in 1995, the NBA, the only major league never to have a strike, may have surged to the top in fan appeal.

Far from the nickel and dime operation when owners operated in small arenas, living on box office receipts and some of the concession income in small markets, the NBA exploded into the big time under Stern. The desire for large TV market cities that dictated the move of Charley's Pistons from Fort Wayne to Detroit, evolved under Stern into TV contracts that led to megabucks and multi-million dollar salaries for the players.

But what pro baseball and football players have forgotten, TV does not really pay their salaries. Team owners in the sports seemed to have

forgotten that too. Fans pay the freight by watching TV as well as paying increasing higher admissions and concession stand prices.

Charley liked a comment attributed to Stern. The commissioner
reportedly said something to the effect that his worst fear is that all the
parties who were essential for the current NBA success will forget how
the league reached its current status. Eckman maintains that the Major
League baseball team owners, with the exception of Peter Angelos, the
principle owner of the Orioles, forgot that in 1994.

Stern did for professional basketball what Pete Rozelle did for the
NFL, another struggling league before and after World War II. Rozelle,
TV and that "Greatest Game Ever Played" between the Baltimore Colts
and the New York Giants in 1958 brought the NFL into the big money.
In gratitude, the NFL owners stuck it to the city of Baltimore, but that's
another story for another time.

Eckman, like his fellow pioneering referees, was there when professional basketball grew in fits and starts. His adventures reveal a part of
the history of the sport from a very unique perspective.

Eckman made $50.00 a game and $5.00 a day meal money. He took
the train from town to town and he rode the "day coaches," and never
got a "sleeper" . . . although his expense account may have shown he
had. He never flew in a plane.

Charley claims that he would wear the same striped referee shirt for
six days or 6,000 miles. When he took the shirt off, it could stand on its
own. His wife, Wilma, says that he really took two shirts on a trip. When
one shirt died, he wore the other. He refereed 158 games in 1948. He
didn't make much and he didn't get paid until August.

Eckman's travels occasionally brought him back home to work
games in the intimate Baltimore Coliseum that was located on Monroe
Street. Once, in his home town, he received a request from a player. The
Lakers were in Baltimore to play the Buddy Jeannette coached Bullets.

Eckman: "It was in the late 40s and before the game, George
Mikan, the Laker star, says to me at mid-court, 'Hey, Charley!
Get me out of here early.' I said, 'What's the matter, George.' He
said, 'Every bone in my body hurts. We're going home tonight
and I want to get up early and go to mass and get the hell out of
town.' I said, 'All right George, I'll take care of it.' He said, 'Make
me look good when you foul me out. Make me look good.'

"We play and, Bingo! Toot, Toot . . . Right there! I give him
the foul call. Toot, Toot! Foul call! I got three fouls on him and

he's laughing . . . smiling . . . snickering. We get to half time. We start the second half and the Lakers are holding Mikan out because of his three fouls. You only got five fouls in those days, just like college ball. Mikan comes back in and, Toot! I blow the fourth foul. One more foul and he's gone. On the fourth foul, he starts to give me some lip. He is leaning over top of me saying, 'What the hell do you mean? I ain't touched this no good Kleggie Hermsen. I ain't never been near him. What the hell are you doing out there?' I said, 'George, what did you say to me?' He said, 'You heard me. You're having a horse shit game!' I said, 'I'm not having half as bad a ball game as you are. But, you aren't going to go. Believe me, you ain't going to leave the game. You're going to stay here all night with me . . . you're going to stay here. I ain't blowin' this whistle no more!'

"Then, Mikan realized what he said to me, 'Oh, no! I didn't mean it, Charley, forget it.' I said, 'No way, George. I ain't blowing the whistle.' I am officiating with Eddie Boyle. I tell him, 'Don't blow the whistle no more on Mr. Mikan. He wants to stay all night.' Man, I got George really hot now. He's looking . . . he's banging guys . . . 'I didn't mean it, Charley . . . I didn't mean it . . .

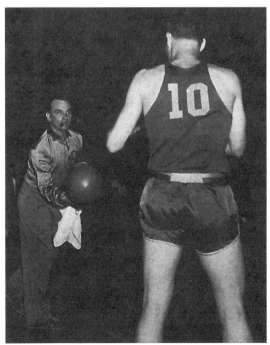

Eckman wipes moisture off the ball before giving it to Chuck Halbert, Washington center. (Photo courtesy of the Baltimore Sun Magazine, *Dec. 10, 1950.)*

Charley, forget it . . . I didn't mean it!' I said, 'Don't worry, George. We'll straighten everything out.' Well, there he goes banging guys. He's hitting them and I ain't blowing nothing. I ain't blowing that whistle. I'm turning my head and talking to somebody on the side line. Man, it gets to be a real rough house.

"We get to the fourth quarter, four or five minutes of play go by, and he says to me 'Get me out of here! I'm dying . . . my knees hurt . . . my ankles hurt . . . For Christ sakes, get me out of here.' So I said, 'Okay, George, get close to somebody.' So, he gets in there and bing!, bang!, bop!, sock! and I blow the whistle. 'Fifth foul and Mikan, you're outahere!'

"Then, Mikan comes by the top of the key and he says to me, 'You know I'm a good Catholic, don't you?' He went to DePaul. He said, 'I want to go to early morning mass.' Now all 6'11" of him is leaning over top of 5'9" me and the fans think he's giving me a lot of lip, right? They are hollering, 'Throw the bum out!' . . . and this and that! I ask him where he is staying and he tells me that he's at the Lord Baltimore Hotel. He is leaning over me all the time with those big glasses on, with that big head, and his 280 pounds. I said, 'Alright, George. You go up one block, and over two to the right and you're at the Cathedral. You can't miss it." And "I'm showing him with the big gestures and it looks like I'm throwing him out of the game. On courtside, the fans, the regulars were hollerin' . . . restaurant owner Bernie Lee, Natie Jacobson, another man about town and a big fan who later owned the old Bullets . . . The fans are going wild . . . I can hear them shouting . . . 'way to go, Eckman . . . throw that big bum out!' All I was doing was telling him how to go to church.

"I gave Mikan directions and he walked out of the game, peacefully, thanking me and he went on about his business. We laughed about it numerous times through the years."

The Circuit Riders

Thanks to the persistence of one of six original referees, Arnold Heft, the National Basketball Association finally recognized the contributions of the pioneer referees.

Eckman: "In 1994, I received a check recently from the NBA for $19,348.00 for past services rendered. Meaning, that we didn't get paid much in those days. There are only six of us still living. Now, its only five, Phil Fox got the check on Tuesday and he died on Wednesday . . . he couldn't stand it. I guess the shock killed him."

As for the others, there was Louie Eisenstein out of Brooklyn; Heft, out of Washington; Sid Borgia from New Jersey; Joe Serafin, from Scranton, Pennsylvania; Kennedy, the head guy; and Eckman.

In those early days of post war professional basketball, these handful of referees became circuit riders. They traveled to the big and small towns of America for not much more than the change you find in between the cushions in your sofa . . . the $5.00 a day meal money is what a cup of coffee costs in some New York City restaurants today. They traveled by train, bus and occasionally flew on DC-3s, a definite museum piece. They stayed at hotels that were built during the Roosevelt administration (Teddy's).

During this period, a fraternity formed. It wasn't a formal organization. It was fused by officiating six games in a week sometimes, sharing meals on that five bucks a day, running up and down the same courts and in small milk run towns called neutral sites, and learning to work together. Charley respected their talents and enjoyed their company.

Pat Kennedy was the supervisor of referees in both the BAA and NBA. Kennedy was a terrific showman. He and Charley worked a lot of games together. Kennedy eventually went with the Harlem Globetrotters and helped Abe Saperstein put on a show.

Eckman: "Kennedy and I refereed the Indianapolis Olympian game one night. Before the game, Kennedy said to me, 'Now, don't get in the way of this Indianapolis club. They come out running. So, get your ass out of there.' Well, I'm on the outside of the court near the sidelines. Then, I go inside to the center of the court, and I'm inside watching the play. "Wah Wah" Jones and the big guy, Alex Groza, are fighting for the ball . . . Groza gets the rebound and, boy, they break down the court. 'Wah Wah' is flyin' down the sideline and Groza gives 'Wah Wah' the lead pass.

" 'Wah Wah' knocks Pat Kennedy flat on his ass about eight rows up into the stands. Kennedy's whistle is flying around in the air. Kennedy is straddled out . . . he don't know where he is at. I'm runnin' down behind them . . . I'm laughing . . . I'm thinkin'

Watching the jump by Halbert, of the Caps, and Red Rocha, of the Baltimore Bullets, at the beginning of a game. Only 5 feet 9 inches tall, Eckman is dwarfed by many of the giant pro players. (Photo courtesy of the Baltimore Sun Magazine, *Dec. 10, 1950.)*

poor Pat may want to stay in the stands for the rest of the game.

"After the game, Pat said to me, 'I'll never go to Indianapolis again. You young guys can run with them.' Pat was a real good fellow as far as I was concerned . . . he was a right guy. He died unexpectedly a number of years back.

"Pat would give out the assignments. In order to get games, Arnold Heft and I would meet Pat in Chicago or St. Louis, or Minneapolis. We would always bring a case of beer to his room or have it sent up . . . and that got us more games the next month. It was as simple as that."

What about the other originals that Eckman worked with?

Eckman: "Sid Borgia, a solid ref, worked the East to the West with me. Sid had a travel bag for all his clothes and it was bigger than him. Usually, we weren't in town long enough to change clothes."

"Phil Fox, a New Yorker, was a great fellow and a fun guy. We called him 'Faintin' Phil.' He was always on his knees begging for mercy or praying or something. Phil was invariably on his knees making a foul call.

"Louis Eisenstein, 'Louie Bluie,' worked with me in the East from time to time. I used to call him 'Wagon Train' because every time we get to the foul line, he would circle me. He would give me the ball and circle me. I would say, 'Would you quit running around me, you're driving me nuts out here.' He was a good guy. We had a lot of fun, Louie and me.

"Louie went West with me once by mistake and he had no hotel room. He had to stay with me. Louie was an Orthodox Jew and he took his prayer shaw . . . his yarmulke . . . he took everything out and he would say his prayers before we would start the game. I said we better be praying good because Sheyboygan was a tough joint to referee in.

"Arnold Heft, from Washington, was a good referee, as good as he wanted to be on any given night. He made some money with what is now the U.S. Air Arena over in Prince Georges County near Washington. He and Abe Pollin, who owns the Bullets and the Washington Caps of the NHL, got together on the arena and I think Heft had to sue Pollin to get his money . . . but he got the money. Heft is now into horse racing. He didn't know a horse from a mule . . . but as soon as he got the money, he became an authority.

"One night, Heft and I are down in a bar in the Loop in Chicago. Heft didn't drink, so he was sitting there near the bartender. The bartender says to him, 'Let me see your watch.' Arnold, who was very proud of his expensive time piece, took it off. The bartender placed the watch on the bar, took a hammer and smashed the watch.

"Well, I thought Heft was going to have a heart attack right there. He hollered and screamed, and jumped. I'm laughing because I seen the bartender do this trick before. Then after Heft got through moaning, and crying and jumping up and down, the bartender gave the real watch back to him and not the one he switched. Arnold's face went from red, to white, to purple to gray."

Joe Serafin often traveled West with Charley and had a habit of having his shoes shined. Asked why, Joe told Charley, "What else are you going to do all day? It's either get my shoes shined or go to a movie. So, I get my shoes shined."

One of the new men Charley broke in was Mendy Rudolph, who traveled with him from East to West. Charley picked him up on his first trip out at the Wilkes Barre, Pennsylvania airport. Mendy later became head referee in the NBA.

Charley had two sets of teeth, his "Lovin' Teeth," that he used in public and when eating and his "Game Teeth" that he used when he was blowing the whistle. He was always concerned that a loose elbow or an errant pass would break his denture and there goes the ball game. While at a restaurant in Milwaukee, they had their coats stolen and with it Charley's "Game Teeth."

Basketball Hall of Famer Buddy Jeannette, who was a player coach for the old Baltimore Bullets said, "Eckman had a barrel of guts. He didn't care if he made a call that brought the house down on him. He made the tough call on the road."

Chapter

6

On the Road Again

*"We played six games in one week in Sheboygan. We had
Denver come in one night and we couldn't leave town because of
the snow and ice and we had to walk to the games. I told those
guys, 'Hey, no fouls. Christ, let's get this thing over with. We
just went through the motions and the score was 144 to 121 . .
. shoot the ball and run . . . and fall back . . . the fans just start
trickling in all day long and night . . . the place held about
4,000 people. That was the greatest town of all . . . Sheboygan."*
—Charles Markwood Eckman,Jr.,
Professional basketball referee

Eckman blazed a trail through the Midwest. He got to know conductors on the trains, the best buys in hotels, and where to get the best T-Bone steaks for the least amount of money. Along the way he stayed at the Hotel Foeste in Sheboygan where one key opened every room.

Joe Hauser, the old first baseman for the International League Orioles had a tavern next to the hotel. He became a friend. Hauser once led the American Association with 63 home runs. Another friend was the elevator operator. When the elevator wouldn't go up, he'd jump off and get the rope and pull that sucker up.

Most nights, Charley went to a town like Moline . . . Rockford . . . Waterloo, Iowa and his partners were "Rent-A-Referees" who usually did college or high school games.

Eckman also learned that style of play varied from West to East. In the East, there always was a lot of contact between the players on the court. It was pick and roll, pick!, pop!, sock! block out! In the West, they would come running, romping and stompin'! It was a different game. It was the same way in the old BAA when Sheboygan was in there with Denver. The Denver guys would run all night, Sheboygan would run . . . and Oshkosh, by gosh, could run. The only team that didn't run that much in the West was the Minneapolis Lakers.

Eckman: "I'll never forget the time we had the Lakers in Denver against the Nuggets and I'm up there refereeing. And I'm running down the floor with the Lakers and Vern Mikkelsen said to me, 'Man, blow that whistle!' I said, 'What's the matter?' He said, 'I can't breath.' We went up and down the first time, the second time nobody's breathin' that rare air, including me. I blew the whistle 'Beep!' 'What happened?,' somebody asked me. 'How the hell do I know, but it was a good idea to stop this mess right here,' I said. And we all got a breather and then we went back to playing basketball . . . it took you a half to get your wind."

Better than the movies

"Better than the movies" was one of Eckman's favorite tag lines. With Charley around, life can in fact seem more like a fantasy than reality. Usually, Charley was the producer, at times, the director. But Eckman never again was the bit player. His cast of characters included the greats, the near greats and not so greats in the world of basketball.

Eckman: "The Philadelphia team had a fellow named Joe Fulks. Joe Fulks was probably the most colorful man in the NBA. He was a big boy from Kentucky, about 6'6", 6'7". The PR guys all lied about the size of their players in those days, but Joe was big and Joe could shoot . . . But he could shoot better if he was half loaded. He would drink that Old Grand Dad whiskey before the game. You would get about half stiff when you talked to him on the court.
. . ."I was refereeing in Philadelphia one afternoon and he said to me, 'Charley, my mother and father in Kentucky are watching me today.' The game was televised in black and white on the old Dumont TV network. Dumont was the first network

*Signaling that
a penalty was
for shoving.*

*This means
one for "giving
him the hip."*

*(Photos courtesy
of the* Baltimore
Sun Magazine,
Dec. 10, 1950.)

*A gesture like this
tells the gallery
that a penalty
Charlie imposed
was for holding.*

to televise the NBA games. So I said, 'Joe, what do you want me
to do?' He said, 'I want you and me to have a beef.' He said 'I am
going to start arguing with you and you get over there near the
camera so my mother and father can see me play for the first
time.' I said, 'Alright, Joe, whatever you want.' What the hell . . .
I don't care. We play about five or six minutes and Joe runs by
me and says, 'I'm going to nail him.' So, he bangs somebody
and I looked at him and I said, 'Oh, Boy!'

   "So now I blow the whistle and Joe comes after me . . . he is
leaning over top of me, giving it to me pretty good and the
cameras are right on us. Joe is saying to me,'Charley, what is
your best side?' I said, 'I'm going to go to my right, Joe' and I

got my finger up in his face and he is hollering and he is getting red faced. He's hollering and I'm hollering and we're doing a square dance around in front of the camera. We go about four or five minutes in front of the camera saying absolutely nothing but, 'How you doing down home? How does it look for you this year? How's your family?' and so forth. We talked about everything but what happened. Now we get through, and I said, 'How's that, Joe?' He says, 'Fine! Let's go!'

"So, I called a foul on him. We shoot the foul shot and I'm running down the floor and about two or three minutes later I go by the Philadelphia bench and Eddie Gottlieb, the coach, is off the bench hollerin', 'Charley, Charley, what the hell is going on? What's that all about?' I said, 'Eddie, Eddie, relax. Ain't nothing going on.' He said, 'What's Joey upset about?' I said, 'He ain't upset. He just wanted to be on TV so his mother and father can watch him. I was helping him, that's all.' Joe was a great guy, by the way. He said, 'I'll buy you a beer tonight.'"

The Start of Something Big

The BAA and the NBL passed the professional referee's whistle to the new league—the National Basketball Association (NBA)—in 1949. Many of the team owners stayed in their home city, but others moved into larger population centers. Ft. Wayne kept a team for a while. Ben Kerner moved the Moline team to St. Louis.

One of the great Eckman stories happened in Indianapolis, where Charley was officiating an NBA game. He nearly touched off a riot. A squawking fan, unhappy that his team was losing to Philadelphia, grabbed a basketball that went out of bounds, taunted Charley with it and then flung it in Eckman's face, knocking out all Charley's front teeth. The guy ran off. Charley jumped the restraining rope in the Butler Field House, caught the guy, and beat the hell out of him. The place erupted.

Maurice Podoloff, then NBA commissioner, told Eckman, "Charley, don't hurt the fans. We don't have enough of them."

An Indianapolis *News* writer, by the way, defended Charley's action. It seems the fan had heckled Charley through out the game. The writer said that Charley was "one of the best officials in the NBA" and should be treated with respect. The writer noted that Charley was calling a good game and was giving the *Olympics* the benefit of the doubt as the home team frequently mugged Paul Arizin, of the Warriors. The writer concluded he felt a lot better now that he defended Eckman in print.

Eckman was picked up in the NBA when it was founded in 1949, along with a cadre of other referees from the BAA. Pat Kennedy was again the Supervisor of officials. In 1951, Kennedy selected Charley as his refereeing partner for the first NBA All Star game ever held. It was in the Boston Garden arena.

Eckman: "Walter Brown, the terrific owner of the Celtics, is the one who thought up the All Star game. Doggie Julian was the coach. He had been the coach at Dartmouth.

"It was exciting . . . fun and you had to live a loose life. You didn't live no life like those guys do today with the planes and private hotel rooms on the road. Nobody was making any kind of money. George Mikan was the big man in basketball in those days. I think he got $27,000 a year at his peak.

"But, about the first All Star game in Boston . . . the basketball writers from around the country wrote that no way in this

After Charley officiated a game at Madison Square Garden, he receives a pin from Stewart Paxton (center), International Association of Approved Basketball Officials. John Nucatola, Supervisor of Eastern Collegiate Athletic Conference Officials, is at right.

God's world could the East team beat the West. The West had the All-Stars from the Minneapolis Lakers, the NBA Champs in 1950 . . . Mikan, Jim Pollard, Vern Mikkelsen, and they had Bobby Wanzer from Rochester. Wanzer could shoot the eyes out of a potato . . . and Bobby Davies, another driver. The East had 'Easy' Ed Macauley, out of St. Louis, the Celtic's Bob Cousy and Bill Sharman. What the writers didn't know was that the West team wanted to get even with George Mikan.

"The game starts and his teammates faked a pass into Mikan and they said go to hell you SOB. They'd throw the ball to each other and they'd shoot. Mikan didn't get the ball. It took the West coach, Johnny Kundla, until almost the entire third quarter of the game before he put in Slater Martin, a good passing guard, to throw the ball to Mikan. Mikan didn't get the ball until then. He was 6'11", the biggest man in the game with a great shot and when he don't get the ball, he don't score. It's hard as hell on you trying to score without the ball.

"Macauley didn't stop him. Mikan's own ball club stopped him because they didn't want him to score . . . they wanted to get even with him because Minneapolis was the power. They were the power in the BAA and now in the NBA."

Professor Eckman

Stanley Frank in the *Saturday Evening Post*, February 19, 1955 wrote, "Referee Eckman always had a penchant for pulling wisecracks. Last season he submitted a report to Maurice Podoloff, president of the NBA, on the progress made by a new referee assigned to work with him. 'I believe he will prove satisfactory to you, since I told him the most important rule to observe in this league,' he wrote. 'I always instruct a new man to hold the ball so that the people in the stands can read your name on it . . . .' "

A Little Fund Raising

With a lack of security in the locker rooms, the referees would give their valuables to a trainer or an equipment manager to hold. Frequently, they would keep their paper money and change in their uniform pants pockets. This was the case, sort of, in Moline one night.

Max Tabacchi was another great ref and a favorite Eckman partner.

Both had been on the road for about two weeks, when they were teamed for a game in Moline. The host Tri-Cities Blackhawks had a charity fund raiser going. The fans were tossing coins on the floor for the crippled kids. About eight or ten little girls on the court were wearing heart shaped canisters. The kids were running around picking up coins and putting the money into those heart shaped buckets.

The game goes down to the wire. With a couple minutes left to play, Moline is getting beat in a tight game. A time out is called. Tabacchi tells Eckman he'll be happy when the game is over because he is tired. With that Max starts to mop his brow with his handkerchief and all of his change falls out of his handkerchief. He had wrapped up his loose coins in a handkerchief before the game started.

> Eckman: "Well, here is Tabacchi . . . as he is mopping his brow all these coins fall out and hit the floor. Well, the fans thought . . . they just knew we had done stolen the coins from those collection canisters. They threw everything at Max from wrappers to chairs. You could have furnished a hotel with the chairs and cushions they had thrown. It took 26 cops to get us off the floor . . . the riot squad came. Tabacchi is over there laughing . . . I'm laughing . . . Tabacchi is trying to get the money off the floor.
>
> "We got through the game. We get in the dressing room and Ben Kerner, the owner of the team, is wild. Kerner was living on a shoestring . . . he had moved to Moline from Buffalo, and he is wild. He's trying to get in the door to get to us . . . banging on the door. Finally, he tries to crawl through the transom . . . he crawls part way through the transom and he is calling us all kinds of names, S.B. this, S.B. that.
>
> "Tabacchi says, 'Hold that door! Don't let that door open!' We were in the dressing room until 1:30 in the morning before we could get out. The fans were out there waiting for us until then, and Kerner was trying to get in after us. It was a beautiful night in Moline."

A casual remark of Charley's overheard by the owner of the Fort Wayne Pistons, Fred Zollner, resulted in Eckman putting his striped shirt in mothballs.

Chapter

7

Driving The Pistons

" 'Charley,' said Fred Zollner, 'is a pistol,' and that is as good a way as any to describe the loquacious leader of the Pistons. Eckman . . . is a kinetic, popgun-talking character with the instincts of a psychologist and the energy of a cheerleader."
— *Murray Olderman,* Sport *Magazine, April 1955*

It never happened before and it hasn't happened since. It was an outlandish idea. What does a referee who never coached basketball before know about coaching, strategy, handling men? The frustrated owner of the Fort Wayne (now Detroit) Pistons, Fred Zollner had watched Eckman referee for a number of years. In a 1955 article entitled "Pro Basketball's Fun at Fort Wayne" in *Sport* Magazine, the well respected sports writer Murray Olderman described how Zollner, a multi-millionaire owner of a piston making factory, had spent an estimated $1 million (a lot of money in those days) trying to bring winning basketball and softball teams to Fort Wayne during a 15-year period. Olderman concluded that since hiring Eckman, the days of losing teams were coming to an end (he was right) along with the red ink associated with losing seasons of the past.

The Hiring

Zollner's interest in Charley developed three years before he actually hired Eckman. According to Olderman's article, Zollner said, "You think

I took a helluva gamble entrusting a team—and a franchise—to a man who had never coached college or pro ball and who was at the time a mere referee? It was no gamble to me. The time had come for a change in Fort Wayne basketball. So I canned the whole front office and took over the operation myself. My next step was to install a coach who I knew could run and nurse-maid a team without any help. I'm busy enough with pistons. Charley was my man. There never was a question of any other.

"As Zollner explained it, his mind was made up as far back as 1951 when he and Charley got together during a post-game party in Milwaukee. 'There were these prima donnas there,' Fred said, 'telling Charley what a great referee he was.' Charley just shrugged. 'I want to be a coach,' he said. I never forgot that statement."

Eckman had just come home after watching the Baltimore Orioles play on the opening day of the 1954 season, which, by the way, was the first Major League game and win in the modern era. Wilma told him that a man from Florida, who would not leave his name, wants Charley to return his call. It was Zollner who asked to meet him the next day in Miami, Florida. Charley had not received the $2,500 the NBA owed him and only had $26.00 in his pocket. In those days, the Eckmans would run

The official team photo of Coach Eckman in 1954.

a tab at the grocery store and pay the bill when the League check came in. He borrowed $50.00 from the grocer for the plane fare to Florida.

A limousine was waiting for him when he landed in Hollywood, Florida. Zollner had a home in Golden Beach. According to Eckman, Golden Beach is about two blocks long with 27 cops in it. Zollner set a meeting for the next morning in the lobby of the hotel. The limo driver takes Eckman to the Kenilworth, a hotel owned by Arthur Godfrey in North Miami Beach. With $6 left, Eckman wondered how he was going to eat in that swanky hotel.

When he arrives, the hotel manager tells Charley that he has a Cadillac at his disposal and to sign for everything. Eckman had never driven a Cadillac before so he gave it a test drive down Collins Avenue. He stopped at *Wolfie's* Restaurant, a popular deli, for a hot dog. Back at the hotel he signs for a fifth of scotch.

At 10 a.m. on Friday, he met Zollner in the lobby.

> Eckman: "Zollner says to me, 'I am going be very brief. I like you personally. I think you could be a coach. I said, 'Well, I do too.' He said, 'You think you could win?' I said, 'I think I could win the pennant with the personnel you've got. I just don't think they have been handled right.' He said, 'That's the same way I feel. I tell you what I'm gonna do. You get along with the players well. They all like you, so I'm gonna make you the coach of the Pistons.' Well, this is unheard of . . . this has never been done before or since. I became the coach of the Fort Wayne Pistons. He says, 'I'm gonna give you $10,000 a year for two years. Do you want to do that?' I said, 'Absolutely! Where do I sign?' $10,000, what are you serious? That's a lot of money in those days. Zollner has one of those public secretaries from the hotel draw up the contract.
>
> "Zollner said, 'This will be for the 1954–55 season. I'm going to give you a bonus every time you win. If you get into the playoffs and win you get $1,500 for each playoff series.' I said, 'That's fine.' I ain't never seen that much money, right? So, he gets through with the contract. I signed it and I said, 'Mr. Zollner, I got to ask you for a favor. The League hasn't paid me and I need some money. How about advancing me $1,000?'
>
> "He said, 'No problem.' He had the secretary get his check book and he gives me a check for 1,000 bucks. Now, I got a $1,000 in my pocket and I'm pretty cockey. He says, 'You get $750 a month all year around. You won't be just doing basket-

ball. You start getting paid next month.' Man, I am living high on the hog. I mean, man, I done died and went to heaven."

Charley called Paul Menton, sports editor of *The Evening Sun,* and Menton put sports writer Walter Taylor on the story from Miami. They never heard of a referee being a coach who never had any coaching experience. On April 15, 1954, the first page of The Evening Sun sports section ran a headline that covered the full width of a full page announcing Charley's selection as the coach of Zollner's team.

Eckman's flight home takes him to the Washington airport. Wilma and a neighbor are to pick him up. Wilma is so excited she locks the keys in the car and they break a window to get in. On the way to Glen Burnie, they stop at Bowie Racetrack so Charley can bet $20 to win and another $20 to show on a horse called "Askauntada." The horse wins and pays $7 for a $2 bet to win. The Eckmans had one heck of a party at home that night.

Eckman: "I didn't have no idea what I was going to do as a coach. But I had the job . . . I was broke and the writers laughed and everybody in Fort Wayne thought Zollner was nuts. People all over the place were saying about Zollner, 'What a dummy!' Everybody wanted the job like Andy Phillip, a great player . . . big George Mikan wanted the job . . . Frankie Brian and a whole bunch of others."

Randy Hooper, The Christian Science Monitor, *April 1955: " . . . But last April when Eckman got a three year contract the whole league was dumbfounded."*

Eckman: "Before I go to training camp, I call Ben Carnevale, the Navy coach. I said, 'Ben, give me a few drills so I look like I know what the hell I'm doing.' He gave me a few drills like two on two, three on two, and that sort of thing. I had to act like I knew what I was doing. But, I knew once I could get into the season, that I could run the ball club. I knew how to substitute, and that the secret of winning in the NBA was matching personnel. I knew that my guy couldn't play this certain player on the other team. I knew if we took another opposition player into the pivot, we could score. I had my own way of doing things, because it's all man for man defense whether you're in Hollywood or on Broadway."

*As Piston coach, Charley, 5'9", gives some last-minute instructions to
Don Meineke, 6'7", before sending Meineke into the game.
(Photo courtesy of* Sports Illustrated.*)*

The Cast of Characters

Charley earned the title of "The Great Communicator" before it was used to describe a certain President of the United States. Coming from the referee ranks to coaching, Eckman thought he should break the ice by visiting each of his players in their homes. His visits paid dividends. He had great respect for Andy Phillip, his field general, who lived in Hollywood. Charley told Phillip that he was counting on him this season. Andy was a smart ballplayer, good ball handler and a good guy to have on the team.

Eckman called George Yardley his "secret weapon". Yardley was little used by the previous Piston coach. The young Forward out of Stanford was surprised when Eckman told him that he would be a starter. Charley knew that the 6'5" Yardley was a great shooter and terrific jumper. Yardley led the League in scoring one year.

Eckman headed south to visit his shooting Guard, Frankie Brian. Brian, whose nephew was Bob Pettit, a star with the St. Louis NBA team, had a great two-hand set shot. Not a defensive player, Brian wanted the ball. He lived in Coushatta, Louisiana, the same home town as the former Baltimore Oriole Catcher Clint Courtney. Joe Adcock, of the Milwaukee Braves, was with Brian when Charley arrived. Eckman maintains that Brian couldn't go to the Men's Room without the ball.

Mel Hutchins, a 6'7" forward from Brigham Young University, was an outstanding defensive player, and a favorite of Eckman's.

Max Zaslofsky, a great star in the BAA and in the early years of the NBA was cut by the New York Knicks. Eckman believed that Max had a couple of years left and persuaded him to join the Pistons. Max had a reputation of being a selfish ball player but while playing for Eckman, Max did everything Eckman asked him to do. He handled the ball, handed off, and he played the pivot.

Charley got Bob Houbregs from the Boston Celtics. Houbregs had also played for the Baltimore Bullets and he would have a key role as the backup center on the team.

A Golden Dome Center

Another piece of the puzzle was the selection of draft choice Dick Rosenthal, the Notre Dame center.

Eckman: "Zollner tells me I gotta' draft Rosenthal. He's 6'5'

Max Zaslofsky (L) with Charley during the 1954-5 season.

and he was going to be a center but I don't know where at. I said, 'How the hell is he going to play center in this league?' Zollner tells me that I got to use him. He sends me up to South Bend to sign Rosenthal for $6,500, but that I could go to $7,000 a year if I had to.

"Zollner tells me he wants Rosenthal, who became the Notre Dame Athletic Director, because he'll get the Catholics to come to the games and the Jewish merchants will support the team because they'll think Rosenthal is Jewish. Zollner says, 'You got to sign him and we will sell the tickets.'

"I go to South Bend and I meet with a guy named Johnny Dee and the priest and then I met Rosenthal. We talked and I said, 'Here's what I can give you. I'll give you a $1,500 bonus, and $5,000 a year.' Dee says Rosenthal is worth more than that. I said, 'Well, gentlemen, this is the only thing I can do for you 'cause I don't really want him. He's 6'5" and there ain't no way he's going to play the Center in the NBA with Mikan at 6'11", and Foust at 6'9" . . . Ray Felix at 7'1". I'm going back to Fort Wayne. If Dick wants to come, have him call me, or come down and see me.'

"The next morning the phone rings. It's Rosenthal calling me from the lobby of my hotel, the Keenen. He said, 'Mr. Eckman, I want to play for you.' We meet. He tells me he's from St. Louis and he has a widowed mother who needs the money. I said, 'I'll send her $500. I'll give you $1,000 and I'll give you a five grand contract.' He said, 'Great! Where do I sign?' Well, I signed Dick Rosenthal, a Notre Dame Center, and I used him as a Guard. But, sure enough, we sold a lot of season tickets."

Perhaps in astonishment, a member of the officiating fraternity, Norman Drucker, admitted that Charley was a pretty decent coach.

Chapter

Let the Games Begin

" . . . Fort Wayne has been hopping around, but that hasn't done the Pistons any harm. Last Tuesday they were here and beat the Lakers with a GREAT rally as Eckman gave Garden fans a terrific show with his hollering and acrobatics on the bench." . . .
— *Leonard Koppett,* New York Post, *December 5, 1954*

Sports Illustrated was fascinated with Coach Eckman. In the January 24, 1955 edition writer Gerald Aster featured Charley in an article titled "Halfway Point in Pro Basketball."

Eckman's style of coaching earned him the nickname "Charley, the Cheerleader." That was only part of his coaching philosophy.

> Eckman: "We finally started the training camp. Now, you only do two things in basketball. You pick and roll . . . you pick and you shoot and if you can shoot and score and rebound you win. If you don't shoot and hit, you lose. It's a very simple game."

Eckman believed that he needed a good chemistry in the clubhouse. Lefty Paul Walther, from Tennessee, didn't play much but was the butt of all the jokes. Everybody made fun of him and he kidded back.

Charley also thought he wasn't in a position to teach his players the fundamentals of dribbling and passing or how to pick and shoot. He said it was essential to the team to get along, match personnel and motivate them.

Strategy

Eckman was the master of match-ups. He probably knew personnel better than any other coach in the League because, as a referee, he saw more players in action than any other coach in the League. Then, he also had these mystic gifts.

Coaching Genius Maneuver

Eckman: "We're playin' the Lakers one night and they had a guy playing for them who had a terrible body odor. My man, Mel Hutchins, a tough defensive player, is playing him. We're 12 points ahead with five minutes to play and this guy gets two baskets in a row. Hell, this guy couldn't throw the ball in the Atlantic Ocean if he was riding on a boat. I called a time out and

Coach Eckman in action. (Photos courtesy of Fort Wayne *Sentinel.)*

said, 'Mel, what in the name of god is going on?' That's not exactly what I said because you gotta talk to your players in their native tongue. You use language that reaches them. I said, 'Get into him . . . get up on him . . . play him tight . . . get up in his chest.' He said, 'Charley, I can't stand his smell and I'm going to throw up.' Now, I'm in the huddle, and I'm saying to myself, 'What the hell am I going to do now.' So I looked around the huddle, and I said, 'Which one of you big clowns can take this guy? I got to have this ball game.' Bobby Houbregs, my 6'8" Center, spoke up, 'Hell, Charley, I'll play him. I got a broken nose. I can't smell nobody.' I put Houbregs on this guy and I won another game because of superior coaching."

Greater Coaching Genius

Eckman: "Larry Foust was a forward when he played at LaSalle, but he was a great Center for me. Foust was on the club for about four years. I would talk to Foust, pat him on the back, tell him he is doing great. 'Biggens' we'd call him and he always wanted to dress like that Matt Dillon on the TV show, "Gunsmoke."

"Anyhow, we're playin' the Boston Celtics. Foust gets a cold one night that turns into a bad case of diarrhea. He says to me, 'Charley, when I raise my hand, get me out of here.' I said, 'Don't worry, Larry. You just come by the bench and tell me to get you out.' He had this diarrhea pretty bad. Now, we're down to a minute left to play and Foust runs by the bench yelling, 'Get me the hell out of here.' I looked down the bench, and I said, 'Quick, Houbregs! Go in for Foust.' The ball goes out of bounds, Foust comes out, Houbregs goes in and Andy Phillip throws the ball to him. Houbregs had a great hook shot . . . a 38-foot hook . . . not no turn around like Kareem Jabar. Bob had a legitimate hook shot . . . it was a bomb. Houbregs takes a step and throws that hook and Bingo! . . . two points for the Pistons.

"Here come the Celtics down the floor, Cousy, Sharman, and Macauley. They shoot and miss. We rebound and kill 10 or 12 seconds off the clock. With a few seconds to play, we throw the ball into Houbregs again and he dumps in another long hook shoot. I'm up on top by three.

"Bob Cousy has the ball for the Celtics. I'm hollering don't

Fort Wayne TV program, 1955. From L to R: Eckman, Fred Zollner, and Hilliard Gates.

touch Cousy. I know he wants to get fouled so they can get the foul shot and maybe beat us. I'm hollerin,' 'Don't touch him . . . get away from him . . . let him lay it in.' Now, he goes the length of the floor trying to bump into anybody and he don't do it . . . so, he lays it in for two. We get the ball, toss in bounds and the game is over. The fans are going wild. What a smart coach! What a tremendous mind! And I'm blowing kisses . . . Wavin' at them . . . Bye-bye . . . Hello, how are you! All because this big guy had to go to the toilet or I get my brains beat out.

"As I am walking off the floor this writer for the Fort Wayne *Sentinel* named Ben Tenney says to me, 'Charley, I've been writing basketball for 48 years and I have never seen a better substitution in my life. How timely. It wins the ball game for you. How did you know when to take out Foust and put in Houbregs?' I looked at him and said, 'Uncle Ben, it's a very simple game. When you got to go, you got to go!' "

Even Greater Coaching Genius

Eckman: "Up in Philadelphia, we're playin' the Warriors. My man George Yardley is on Paul Arizin. Arizin had a tendency to go coughing like he had asthma. It seemed like he was always spitting or coughing on you. He's shooting over Yardley and he made four baskets in a row. I called time out, and I said, 'What in the world is going on, George? Why don't you get in close to Arizin. Why don't you play him up tight? He's not that quick.' George said, 'Charley, he's spitting all over me.' I said, 'Oh, Jesus!' I got the water boy to bring me some water. I said to Yardley, 'Here, before you go out there drink this water but don't swallow. When you get close to Arizin, spit on the son of a bitch.' So, he gets back in the game. Arizin comes up on him and George spits on him. Now Arizin backs up. He's already got enough germs, so he figures he don't want to get any more. Yardley gets 31 points that night and we beat Philadelphia bad. It was a helluva a night. Arizin snotting at Yardley and Yardley spitting at Arizin."

New York Cabbie Genius

Eckman: "We used to play double headers in Madison Square Garden. I get off the plane from Dayton, Ohio and I get into the cab at the airport. The Pistons are playing the second game of the double header against the Knicks. I said: 'Take me to the Garden' In those days, everybody spoke English in New York and the cabbie said: 'Ah, you like basketball?' I said: 'Well, I ain't going there to dance.' He don't know I'm the coach of the Pistons. We get to the Garden and I pay him the fare. He asks me how much money I have left. I tell him I had about $75.00. He said to me, 'Well, listen. You look like a right guy. You meet Big Sam by the escalator in there. He's got a red shirt on and take the Pistons.' I said, 'Are you serious? The Knicks are five or six point favorites.' He said, 'Look, buddy, take the Pistons tonight. They will win by one.'

"I said to myself ain't this awful he don't know who I am . . . he thinks I am a spectator. I don't look like a coach, right! After I give him a tip, he tells me to have a night on the town after the game and that I should call him in the morning if I wanted to go back to the airport.

"At half time, I'm losing by 38 points. We get rollin' in the third quarter. We're down by 12 by the end of the Quarter.

"With a minute to play in the game, we're tied. We got a jump ball at the top of the key. Mel Hutchins gets the tap and hits the ball to George Yardley. Yardley fakes and passes to Frankie Brian. Brian lays it in for two and gets fouled. He makes the foul shot. Now, I'm three on top and I'm off the bench screaming . . . I got my coat off . . . I throw my coat away. I'm soaking wet.

"Here come the Knicks down the floor. They throw the ball in to Connie Simmons. He takes a hook shot—two points. Here we come down the floor and, Bingo! Andy Phillip gets fouled. He makes the shot. We're back on top by two. Dick McGuire has got the ball for the Knicks and I'm hollering hit him . . . foul him . . . do anything, but hit him. Well, we get him and he makes his foul shot. We throw the ball in bounds and the game is over. We win the game by one after being down by 38. The place is going crazy . . . 18,000 nuts up there in the Garden.

"I look up at the score board and I think, 'That cab driver told me I would win by one.' I'm starting to laugh. The great writer from the New York Post, Milton Gross, comes to me and asks what the hell is going on, 'Why are you cracking up? You won a big ball game. You beat the Knicks by one and you're in first place by four and a half games. What the hell are you laughing at?'

"I said, 'Milton, forget it. It's a very simple game. Hell, the cab driver who drove me in from the airport today told me the Pistons were going to win by one. They don't need me out here.' Gross got to laughing so hard he wasn't no more good the rest of the night."

Actual Genius

Eckman: "If I had a real good shooting guard there were times I'd take the center out. I did that with several players. I did that with Zaslofsky and Dick Rosenthal, a college 6'5" center, against the Minneapolis Lakers. We beat the Lakers six straight games in 1954–55. The Lakers don't beat me even with a bunch of great players like Vern Mikkelsen and 6'9" Clyde 'Jelly Belly' Lovellette, a big hook shooter. I would run Rosen-

1954-55 NBA Western Division Champs. Top row (L to R): "Lefty" Walther, Andy Phillip, Dick Rosenthal, Max Zavlofsky, Frank Brian, Phil Olofson. Second row: Otto Adams, Charley Eckman, E. Simmons, W. Painter, Stan Kenworthy, Third row: Bob Houbregs, Larry Foust, George Yardley, Don Meineke, Mel Hutchins.

thal, my guard, into the pivot and Whitey Skoog would have to guard him. Whitey had a bad right knee, and he couldn't play Rosenthal. In order for me to put Rosenthal in the pivot, I had to take Larry Foust out. Larry didn't like to come out of the pivot. When anybody came through there, he hit them in the head with the ball. So, I had to take him out of the game and put in my substitute center, Bobby Houbregs, to play forward.

"Houbregs would take his man outside and Rosenthal would go inside. Rosenthal would get Skoog in foul trouble. Dick would throw a hook shot or two and Bingo! He was a natural center but Rosenthal wasn't fast enough to be a good guard against good fast guards or big enough to play center. But he could play against a fellow like Skoog and that's called matching personnel. Well, that one maneuver won me six ball games against the Lakers and won me a pennant."

After he was named Athletic Director at Notre Dame, Dick Rosenthal came to Baltimore to speak to the Maryland Chapter of the Alumni Club. Rosenthal acknowledged to sports columnist John Steadman, "It was fun being with Charley. He made a guard out of me and he was a master at matching up our personnel with the opposition."

During Charley's first year as coach, he and play-by-play broadcaster Hilliard Gates developed a mutual admiration. Gates showed his feelings in his December 1954 column in the Fort Wayne game program.

"The news that Charley Eckman had officially received the bid to coach the West All Stars in the annual NBA All Star classic certainly was welcome. It's doubtful if anyone has ever worked harder at the job given him than the present coach of the Pistons. When one realizes that he had virtually no previous coaching experience and in a short time has molded a squad that is setting the pace, Eckman's performance is even more remarkable.

"There is no question that never before in the history of major sports competition has a 'rookie' coach been able to win the distinction of piloting an All Star organization. It is an honor that Eckman didn't seek—other than by indirection—yet we know he must be extremely proud of the selection.

"Charley—in accepting the bid—credits his players with providing the honor. Eckman has never sought personal glory for the manner in which the Pistons are playing. Last Saturday night—following the Rochester triumph—we walked into the Z dressing room. We extended a hand of congratulations to Eckman. He turned to the players and said, 'Congratulate these guys. I haven't made ONE basket all season.' "

Eckman did it once. Was it a fluke, or could he do it again?

And the Winner is . . .

"As far as the other coaches are concerned, the appointment of Eckman (as coach of the Pistons) was a bad joke.
"But the joke was on everyone else"
— Leonard Koppett, Championship NBA (1954–55 Review)

The Piston's rise to the top of the West was accompanied by the generally admiring glare of an incredulous sports media. Some writers suggested, however, that Eckman had more than his coaching genius going for him. They implied that he had something "higher" going for him . . . or perhaps "lower."

The Power of Z

With Eckman's Pistons beating the Lakers like a drum, the Minneapolis team wouldn't play Fort Wayne at home. One night in Minot, North Dakota, during a terrible storm with sleet and snow, the Pistons win by one. Zollner made the trip in his two-engine DC-3 airplane, "The Flying Z."

Zollner insists that the team is going to fly out of Minot when nothing else was flying, not even the birds. Two World War II ex-fighter pilots were the captains, Jack Cooney and Bob Novak. They warm up the plane in the hangar and everybody gets on.

Also on the plane are the refs, Louie Eisenstein and 'Jocko" Collins,

two or three writers and, in Charley's opinion, the best play-by-play basketball broadcaster, Hillard Gates. The plane roars out of the hangar
hell bent for leather and takes off. The plane is bouncing around in the
air. The plane didn't have any oxygen so the highest it could fly was
10,000 feet.

Eckman: "At 7,500 feet, we're bouncing down the highway.
Zollner and I were sitting in the back of the plane and the players are up front. The players are throwing up and laying on the
floor like they're dying. 'Jocko' is so sick he's crossed himself
and he's saying prayers from his prayer book while fingering his
beads. Louie Eisenstein gets his prayer shawl out . . . he's got
his yarmulke on, and he's prayin'.

"Captain Cooney comes back and he says, 'Fred, Fort

*1955-56 Western Division NBA Champs, just after winning a semi-final
play-off series from the St. Louis Hawks. After losing two games of the
five-game series, the Pistons stormed back to win three straight.*

Wayne's airport is closed and we've got to decide if we should turn back or go ahead.' Zollner puffs on his cigar and he asks Cooney how long do we have before making a decision. Cooney says we have about eight minutes. Zollner says, 'I'll take care of it from here in. You just go fly the plane and come back in eight minutes.'

"Zollner looks at me and then he starts stomping on the floor, and he says, 'Hello, D . . . This is Z . . . Hello, D . . . This is Z . . . Hello, D . . . This is Z . . . Open it up down there.' So, Louie Eisenstein says to him, 'Mr. Zollner, to whom are you speaking?' Zollner says, 'I'm talking to the devil. Who the hell do you think I'm talking to.' Louie says, 'Why are you talking to the devil? Why don't you talk to Jesus? At least he is one of our boys.'

"Zollner says, 'Let me tell you something, Louie. Everybody down there at night is praying Dear Lord, give me this . . . Dear Lord, give me that. Louie, you only talk to the Lord when it's a clear night, bright skies, blue clouds, and everything is nice and rosey. That's when you talk to Jesus Christ. The devil put this shit up here. Let him get rid of it. Hello D this is Z . . . open it up down there.'

"Captain Cooney comes back in eight minutes and says, 'Fred, Fort Wayne opened up. It's 600 feet and we're going in.' We land the plane. Eisenstein gets off and kisses the ground. He has his prayer shawl around him. He put that on the ground and kissed it. 'Jocko' Collins says he'll never fly with us again and if he ever sees Zollner again it will be too soon.

"I'm the coach, right! What do I say. 'Great flight!' I mean, we landed, what the hell do you want. We're the only thing that flew in the whole midwest that night. But that's the way Zollner believes—the devil for bad things and Jesus Christ for good things. I can't fault his philosophy."

Down to the Wire

Fort Wayne didn't know what to make of him. He was a winner, something the Fort Waynians weren't used to. But their surprise paled in comparison to the shock wave that struck the basketball wise guys and the entire NBA. In his first year as coach, Eckman and his team made the play-offs.

Eckman: "We opened the play-offs in Fort Wayne. We lose the first game because Frankie Brian didn't see Mel Hutchins under the basket . . . or he saw him and wanted to dribble in and lay it up. He misses the lay up and, man, the place goes ape.

"We get beat again in St. Louis. We come back to Fort Wayne and I tell my team we have to have this ball game. Everybody on the team put out and we beat them by 10 or 12 points. St. Louis thought they would win the pennant at home . . . beat our brains out. They had Charley Share . . . they had Bob Pettit . . . and they had that Jack McMahon, who was a good guard. They had a pretty good ball club. Red Holzman was the coach. Red, a former University of Baltimore player who played with the Rochester Royals, and a good guy, later coached the New York Knicks to the world championship.

"We go back to St. Louis and I take Mel Hutchins aside. I tell him that I booked a private room for him for the night and I told him that I wanted him to be by himself. I told him. 'We need to win this game tomorrow. I want you to play Pettit. Hutch, I got to have this game.' He says. 'OK, Chas, don't worry. I'll take him.'

"Pettit was about four inches taller than Mel Hutchins, but Mel had great reflexes. He was the best defensive player in the league until Bill Russell came along. The next night, we go out on the floor and Mel takes Pettit. I put Foust on Charley Share. These were pretty good match ups. Pettit figures he's got a "piece of pie" 'cause he could jump over Hutchins.

"There's thunder and lightning coming and going through the sky as we go to the arena. We had thunder and lightning on the court that night. Hutchins held Pettit, a scoring machine, to nine points. Foust is killing Share and we beat them by 14 points, in St. Louis, in that blinding storm. This was a big game, bigger than anything you could imagine at that time."

The Power of Z Again

Eckman: "We flew to St. Louis on 'The Flying Z,' Zollner's private plane. I said, 'Aren't we going to stay in St. Louis tonight, Fred? It's bad up there.' Zollner had an appointment the next day and we flew out in that storm. I mean we bounced all the way to Fort Wayne. We were plenty loose all right . . . loose and scared.

Charley is hoisted by some of his winning players after they defeated the East 108-94 in the 1956 NBA All-Star Game. L to R: Bobby Wanzer, Charley, and George Yardley.

"We had the next night off, and the following night we played St. Louis in Fort Wayne. I had my team as high as a Georgia Pine. We beat them by 30 some points. That win gave us the championship of the Western Division."

An Avis Finish

The Pistons had to face the winners of the Eastern Division, a terrific Syracuse team lead by Dolph Schayes. The city of Fort Wayne was so supportive that the coliseum, a beautiful building, was rented out to a bowling conference because the powers that be didn't think the Pistons would win with Eckman as the coach. With no home court to play in, the Pistons were forced to schedule their three home games in Indianapolis.

Eckman: "We played two games in Syracuse and get beat and we go to Indianapolis, a foreign court. We beat them three in a row the hard way. We go back to Syracuse. By the end of the first half, I got Syracuse beat by 17 points. Frankie Brian didn't like a call by Louie Eisenstein . . . he gives Louie a lot of lip. Louie calls a technical foul, and, Bingo! They got momentum and they beat me by three or four. They should never have beat me that night. We should have won the world championship. The next night, they beat us again and Syracuse wins the championship. We went seven games.

"We flew home to Fort Wayne. The fans are out there waiting for us at the airport at 3:00 in the morning . . . we make speeches . . . we throw kisses . . . a great night!"

Charley was a winner—a celebrity in a city that was starved for a basketball winner. A Fort Wayne company, the Eddale Corporation, was so delighted that in 1955 it created a basketball board game, "Home

Fort Wayne holds Appreciation Night for Charley in 1955. Wilma and Charley receive gifts and applause.

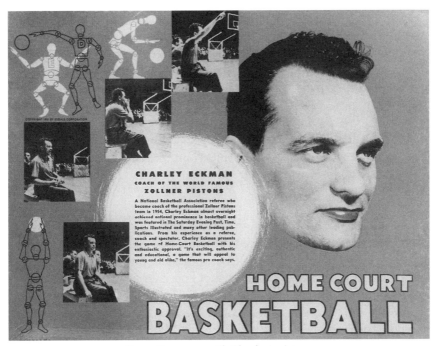

Game Box cover with Charley's picture.

Court Basketball", with Charley's picture on the cover of the box. While it never reached the popularity of *Monopoly, Clue* or *Chutes and Ladders*, the game sold very well in Fort Wayne.

Charley finished the season with the most victories (43) of any coach and was named the NBA Coach of the Year. He was rewarded with a bonus of $4,500 and a new Oldsmobile. He signed a new three year contract starting at $12,500 (a lot of money in those days). That was the first year.

Eckman claims that he should have finished second because the worst thing he did was win that first year.

> Eckman: "In professional sports, when you win that first year, you better darn sight be ready to win the second and third year or you're gone. The second year we won the pennant again, and I got another raise. Now I was making $15,500 a year. The third year we tied for second place."

In Terry Pluto's "Tall Tales," George Yardley, Eckman's scoring machine said, "Charley is exactly what we needed. Paul Birch (the former Piston coach) was a drill sergeant. Charley's greatest attribute was that he treated us as human beings. He rolled the ball and let us play . . . We got to the finals two years in a row, then Fred (owner Fred Zollner) started trading everyone . . . By the end Charley had nothing to work with." In 1957–58, Yardley led the league in scoring with a 27.8 average.

For the 1956–57 season, Eckman traded Ron Sobie to the New York Knicks for former University of Maryland All-American guard Gene Shue. Shue had been signed by Philadelphia and quickly traded to the Knicks.

Eckman: "New York didn't know what they had. I knew this kid from Towson Catholic, his high school, and Maryland. He was skinny for a pro and a little homesick, but he could score. He had a great two handed set shot and later added a one handed jump shot. I got his high school sweetheart from Bawlemore out to Fort Wayne so they could get married. That solved the homesick problem and then I turned him loose on the court. It's a very simple game!"

Shue became one of the best scoring guards in the NBA, coached a number of teams and is the Director of Player Personnel with the Philadelphia 76ers. He has said publicly that Charley gave him the biggest break in his career by trading for him. Shue said that this allowed him to settle in with one team. He added, "Charley knew me and had a lot of respect for how I played. Charley gave me a great opportunity."

In a footnote to professional basketball history, *Sport's Illustrated*'s article on the Detroit Piston's owning its own jet airplane, reader Neil Baron of East Lansing, Michigan wrote noting that Zollner made history with his DC-3, "The Flying Z". *Sport's Illustrated* printed a photo of the team emerging from the airplane in the February 1992 issue.

The fourth year was a bummer!

10

Coaches are Hired to Be . . .

Loose was Eckman's style. The game was close and time was running out. Eckman called a time out. The team surrounded him waiting to hear Charley's strategy. One asked, "You got a play?" Charley said, "Kid, there's only two plays—'South Pacific,' and put the ball in the basket."

Auto Pits Weren't the Only Pits in Detroit

In the fourth year of his coaching reign, the wheels fell off Eckman's Piston Express when the franchise moved to Detroit. Many fans thought Charley was behind the move to the Motor City and he felt the heat. Piston (the stuff made of metal) King, Fred Zollner, wanted to be near his prime customer, General Motors.

In truth Charley loved Fort Wayne and didn't want to leave. He considered Fort Wayne a great basketball town that deserved a team. But, the NBA wanted to go to the bigger markets and Zollner had to go with the league. TV was coming on strong as a financial resource for the NBA and everybody was making moves. All the small basketball towns were out of the picture . . . Waterloo . . . Moline . . . Rochester . . . Syracuse were all finished.

Eckman returned to Fort Wayne in 1977 to speak before the Grocery Manufacturers Retail Association meeting. As reported in the *Fort Wayne Sentinel*:

"20 Years Later, Eckman Tells It Like It Was

"He's 20 years older, a few pounds heavier and probably a little wiser but he hasn't slowed down any. Charley Eckman, who traded his referee's whistle for the pressures of coaching is back in Fort Wayne today—the first visit since he followed the Fort Wayne Pistons to Detroit in 1957.

"There were those 20 years ago who said Charley led the charge to Detroit, that he was the prime force behind Fred Zollner's decision to make the switch. 'That's a lot of . . . ' Charley will tell you. And that's what I'm going to tell them (the Grocery Manufacturers Retail Association) tonight. I took a bad rap,' Charley chatted while having dinner at John Ceruti's, an old friend from the old days.

" 'I was treated better here in Fort Wayne than any place I'd ever been,' continued Charley as as he twirled his cigar around in his mouth. 'And who are we kidding? I was making $15,000 and Fred's got millions. Am I going to tell him what to do?' "

". . . 'You know what really happened? Fred told Mr. Adams (Otto) to tell me what to say. And I said it. But it wasn't my idea.' Hell, if I wanted to move the club I'd have picked Cincinnati, some place where I could get some ball players. Oscar Roberston on a territorial draft. How many ball players did you get out of Detroit in those days? Hell, I liked Fort Wayne. My family liked it here. And I've got nothing but good memories. It's great to be back here again,' Charley continued in his harsh, rapid-fire manner."

Eckman was convinced that with Roberston he would have been a winning coach for many more years. This is based on the theory that players make coaches. Coaches don't make players.

Eckman: "Zollner wanted to go into the big time. Well, we went into the big time . . . Detroit. The citizens of Detroit could have cared less if we were in town. They had the Lions in football and the Tigers in baseball. The hockey team, the Red Wings, were doing good, and so we had no place to practice. We wound up in Cobo Arena. It was brutal with slippery floors . . . we couldn't practice.

"I got a new three year contract. I'm staying in the Cadillac hotel and I got Bill Veeck, who was a real baseball promoter, and I got the legendary Tiger great Mickey Cochrane, the old catcher, working for me as salesmen. Veeck was going to do public relations work. At the time, Veeck was working for the Baltimore based National Bohemian Brewery. National Boh had bought a brewery in Detroit. I selected National Boh as the sponsor of our radio broadcast, instead of taking Strohs Bohemian.

"I went with National because of my home-town connections. I figured it would help me get a job after I got through with basketball 'cause you know you are going to get fired sooner or later. Of course, I got fired but the job with National didn't pan out.

"Now, we are in Detroit and we get pretty lousy fast. We had a terrible time of it on the court. I think we lost 12 out of 15 or 16. When Yardley got hurt, I lost my shooter. Foust had about had it. I had to trade Phillip and Hutchins on boss's orders. I didn't want to get rid of Mel Hutchins. Zollner made me get rid of him because he thought Mel had been in business with Jack Molinas, the player who was convicted in the college point-shaving scandal. I don't think Mel was . . . I never did and I feel that way to this day. Mel Hutchins did more for that club than anybody else. I guess Hutchins never knew why he was traded until he reads it in this book. Zollner insisted I trade him to New York. He played about eight games for New York and got hurt."

The trade brought Harry "The Horse" Gallatin, Nate "Sweetwater" Clifton, and Dick McGuire from the Knicks. Gallatin and Clifton were great guys, according to Charley, but past their prime. McGuire was still a terrific ball handler, but he wasn't a shooter. Eckman now had no strong defensive player and no shooter. He and his team were on a runaway train heading down hill without brakes . . . and the bridge was out.

The Bitter with the Sweet

Eckman: "Being around 'Sweetwater' Clifton was better than the movies. We went on speaking engagements and personal appearances in towns Rand McNally never heard of. We come back from one trip and there were about six women sitting in the lobby of the Cadillac Hotel in Detroit. I said, 'Who are these ladies, Sweets?' He said they are all his ex-wives.

"Well, each one of them wanted money. So I cashed a check for $3,000, and gave each one of them $500. I said, 'Sweets,' how do you want to pay for this?' He said, 'You just saved my life. I don't care how you take it out of my paycheck, just leave me have some spending money.' He was getting $8,500 a year so we took it out of his paycheck a couple hundred a month.

" 'Sweets' was a hell of a guy . . . a real great guy. Any time a fight started, or when anybody would start shoving and pushing and getting nasty, I would send 'Sweetwater' Clifton out to the middle of the floor and all the fighters became lovers . . . because if 'Sweetwater' Clifton hit you, he could have killed you. They all knew it. They didn't fool with 'Sweets.' "

The Pistons move to Detroit and obtain new players. L to R: Walter Dukes, Charley, club official, and "Sweetwater" Clifton, 1958.

Another Phone Call from the Boss

Eckman: "A month and a half or two, after the season started, Zollner called me up from Florida. We had just come back from getting beat by St. Louis by 20 points. He asks, 'How did you do last night?' Like he don't get no papers in Miami. I said, 'We got beat.' He said, 'What's the matter with the team?' I said, 'Well, hell, we got a pretty bad ball club. I got to rebuild. Yardley is hurt and I don't have anybody to shoot the basketball. We're not going anywhere.' He said, 'I think we'll make a change in your department.' I said, 'Yeah, Fred, who are we going to get rid of?' And then I realized I was the only son of a bitch in my department. He said, 'I'll pay you for this year and next and you are gone.' I enjoyed it and I thanked him for the opportunity. But that's how I got fired because they had nobody else in my department but me. Today, the coaches got four guys on the bench telling them what to do.

"That was the end of my coaching career. I came back to my home in Glen Burnie, Maryland. I took a year off and then I went back to refereeing the Atlantic Coast and other Conferences and stayed there for 10 years as a referee. I worked all the playoffs, the NIT, the NCAA, and I had some great times. My record as a coach wasn't too bad—two pennants . . . I tied for second and got fired in the fourth . . . and I was the winning coach of an NBA All-Star Game."

Not too bad? I guess not. In the years 1954–1957, he compiled the most victories in the '54–'55 season, the most Division Championships during the period '54–'57, and was second only to "Red" Auerbach in total victories over those years. "Red" only surpassed Charley after the Celtics obtained Bill Russell. The record is even more remarkable considering that it took the Pistons another 32 years before they won a championship.

Now for Charley, it was back to the future . . . officiating college basketball. A reporter once wrote that the best investment Eckman ever made was the 50 cents Charley spent to buy his first whistle.

Chapter

11

Charley's Ballroom

"I had been officiating a St. John's game one night in the Garden. Dick McGuire, a great playmaking Guard who I got later to play for me with the Pistons, was having a terrible time shooting foul shots. Before every shot he would cross himself, but he missed five straight foul shots. Just before the half ended, McGuire missed two more foul shots. He is a good guy and a devout Catholic. As we are walking off the floor, this priest leans over the railing and he says, 'Can I talk to you a minute, Dick?' Dick says, 'Sure, Father. What can I do for you?' He says, 'Dick, I know you are a good Catholic. I know you are very sincere, and I appreciate that. But, would you do me a favor for the whole religion?' Dick says, 'Sure, Father. What's that?' 'Don't bless yourself any more,' he said, 'You keep missin' those foul shots and you're making the religion look bad!' McGuire would have liked to have died."
—*Charles Markwood Eckman, Jr., Referee*

Eckman's Ballroom is his world of basketball. Everywhere he worked a court, in high school gyms, at colleges and in the pro ranks, was his Ballroom. He worked in scruffy little gyms and the meccas of the game . . . and along the way he had a hell of a lot of fun. Before and after his coaching career, Charley handled college games with his usual flare.

Sport's Illustrated writer Frank Deford wrote in 1976, "Eckman has made it as a personality as he did as an official, simply by being himself. 'Handling people is three-fourths of refereeing,' he says. 'All these yo-yos these days take it too seriously.' Once, before a tense NIT final at Madison Square Garden, he showed up on the court in dark glasses. College kids would drop by after games they had lost and thank him for a nice fun game."

A Couple of Bites from the Big Apple

Eckman: "I loved to referee in Madison Square Garden in New York. You could hear them fans all hollering. When I first went up to the Garden as a young man, I was refereeing a game and this loud mouth sucker is sittin' by the side line. He's bellowing, 'You stink . . . you SOB . . . this and that . . .' I walked over by the Scorers' Table and I looked up at this guy and I said 'Did you pay to get in?' He said, 'I paid $20.' I said, 'Good! I'm getting $100 to be out here. Now, who's the dummy?' That stopped that bastard. He got up and left the building."

Ned Irish ran the Garden. According to Charley, Lester Scott, the Public Relations chief, was first class. The old Madison Square had a great atmosphere for basketball. Teams knew they were in the big time when they played in "The Garden".

No Whistle

Twenty-two thousand fans jammed Madison Square Garden to see two of the country's best teams, St. John's and Holy Cross, square off for number one ranking in the nation and bragging rights among Catholic colleges, the top teams on the hardwood 30 years ago. This was the big one—the championship game of the National Invitation Tournament (NIT), bigger in those days than the NCAA tourney. Eckman would be assigned Tuesday, Thursday and Saturday games. He would work the finals and he would stay the entire week in New York. He received $75 a game and expenses.

For this war, he worked along with another, not so seasoned referee from upstate New York.

Eckman: "I could tell from the start that this guy was

chokin'. He didn't blow the whistle the whole first quarter. Just like ballplayers, referees choke up, but the NIT was a hell of a place for it to happen. The joint was rockin', no doubt about it, and he was intimidated by the crowd.

"He came over to me during a break in the action and said, 'I can't blow the damn whistle.' I told him not to worry about it and to just call out of bounds and jump balls, that I'd take care of the rest. He seemed relieved and everything was goin' along fine through the whole game and then, with the score tied and 30 seconds to play, it happened.

"He was the lead official on the play. We had two refs in those days, a lead official and a trail official. As play moves back and forth on the floor, the roles are switched. The lead becomes the trail and vice versa. So he's in closer than me to a bunch of action where the big guys are crashin' the boards and he blows the whistle.

"So I'm waitin' and 22,000 fans and all the players and coaches are waitin' and nothin' happens! I run over to him and ask, 'Are you alright? Whataya got?'

"He looks at me and says, 'I ain't got shit. I can't blow the whistle.' Well, the son-of-a-bitch just blew it and we got 22,000 fans ready to hang both of us from the rafters unless one of us shows he's got balls!

"As I'm assessing the situation, I look over and see a couple of guys from one team gettin' up off the floor near the foul line and there's a big, gawky kid from the other team standin' nearby. He was probably the biggest player on the floor.

"So I rush over to where he's standin' and yell, 'That's it! Youuu! Number 22! Put up your hand!'

"He looks at me and says, 'Who hit 'em? Not me! I didn't hit anybody.' So I says, 'Who the hell do you think hit'em? Put your hand up!' He stops questioning me, raises his hand and nobody in the crowd knows the difference.

"To this day, I believe I talked that big, gawky kid into thinkin' he fouled somebody."

Nuturing the Garden

The NIT had great teams and great rivalries . . . St. Johns . . . LaSalle . . . Providence College with Johnny Egan and Lenny Wilkens, who became a successful coach in the NBA. John Thompson, the coach of the Georgetown team, was a center on the team. Providence was a powerhouse in those days.

Eckman: "St. Johns always had good solid teams when Joe Lapchick and Frank McGuire coached there. There was Niagara with their coach 'Taps' Gallagher, one of the finest men I ever met. St. Bonaventure's would be invited. They had a pretty good ball club. And you would have the St. Louis University Billikens . . . that's when I first met Bob Ferry. He later became General Manager of the Bullets. His son, Danny, was an All-American at Duke. Danny has made a name for himself in the pro ranks. Holy Cross was always tough with Cousy and George Kaftan."

Niagara, coached by "Taps" Gallagher, a good Catholic, goes against Temple coached by Harry Litwack, who is of the Jewish faith, in the Holiday Festival during the Christmas college break in the Garden. Eckman and Hal Grossman are officiating the game. Grossman reports, "We walked onto the court and Charley goes over to 'Taps' and says, 'No sweat, no sweat, 'Taps,' you got me. But I would worry about that son-of-a-bitch, Grossman, because he has Litwack.' I said, 'This game might be a draw.' 'Taps' starts to laugh. I tell Harry what Eckman said and he starts to laugh. Now, the coaches were loosey, goosey, and we have an easy game."

Alabama Bound

Eckman: "I was refereeing a University of Alabama ballgame in the Garden one night. Alabama had this little guard, Lenny Kaplan. He is hitting these big farmers from Alabama in the back of the head with the ball . . . he's hitting them in the knee cap. He threw the ball in bounds faster than a speeding bullet. His own team didn't know what hit them. The other team wasn't beating him and he could do what he wanted to do. . . . and he was scorin' a lot of points. He could run like a deer and he could shoot the ball . . . a good two hand-set. I thought he was quite an athlete.

"I ran along side of him and said, 'Hey, Kaplan! I don't know what you are doing but I'm going to tell you this much . . . my train leaves at ten-forty . . . and I better be on it heading to Baltimore, because I got to go to work tomorrow morning. I don't want to see no tricks.' He said, 'Don't worry, Mr. Referee. You'll be on that train.' And he was right. I was on that train.

"Lenny later married one of the daughters of Leon Shavitz. In the old days, Shavitz ran the most popular delicatessen in Baltimore, 'Nate's and Leon's,' at North and Linden Avenues. Lenny ran a legendary restaurant started by his father-in-law for many years, 'The Pimlico Hotel,' and he is still in the business with the 'Polo Lounge' . . . a first-class joint in Baltimore across from The Johns Hopkins University."

Smokin' with Charley on Tobacco Road

Everett Case, the North Carolina State Coach, pushed to have Eckman return to officiating in the Atlantic Coast Conference (ACC). Charley considered the ACC the best he ever worked. Great teams make for great rivalries . . . North Carolina, North Carolina State, Maryland, Wake Forest, Clemson and Duke—college powerhouses with great coaches through the years. Charley worked the playoffs every year.

Getting Up

Eckman and Hal Grossman were scheduled to work the ACC final. The night before, they are invited to a University of Virginia party that lasted into the wee small hours. Looking slightly rumpled when they arrived, Duke coach Vic Bubas hollers at them, "How you gonna get up for the game?" Eckman answered, "Don't worry, Vic. I've been up all friggin' night!"

Preventing A Homicide

Once upon a time, South Carolina was a member of the ACC. In Charley's era, South Carolina had a legendary coach in the late Frank McGuire. South Carolina squared off against North Carolina State and its coach Norm Sloan (who had succeeded Everett Case). Eckman and Hal Grossman were assigned the game. Earlier in the week, Grossman was part of the mixed conference officiating crew between N.C. State and Indiana. During that game, N.C. State's coach, Sloan, and Grossman had a few words. Tempers had barely cooled between Sloan and Grossman for this crucial match between McGuire's Gamecocks and

ACC Tournament referees receive trophies from Commissioner in '50s. L to R: Lou Bello, Phil Fox, Louie Eisenstein, Commissioner, Charley, and Red Mihalik.

Sloan's Wolfpack. Within the first two minutes of the game, Sloan's big mouth and Grossman's tenderized ears resulted in two technical fouls against Sloan and a game ejection . . . with a big "You're out of here!" gesture from Grossman.

The double toot brought Eckman flying across court and gesturing wildly to halt the action and hollering "Whoa, Baby, Whoa Baby!" McGuire, on the South Carolina sideline, is loving it. He is wearing a Mona Lisa smile, but the meaning is clear. 12,000 thousand nuts in the stands are going crazy.

Charley stood in front of Hal, arms locked shoulder height, chin out and legs spread, and inquired, "What the —— is goin' on here?" Hal explained that for the second game in a row, Sloan had gone way above and beyond the call of referee baiting and that he, Hal, had had enough. Eckman, "But the damn game is only a couple of minutes old. You throw Sloan out and we ain't getting out of here alive." Grossman says "Do you mean that?" Eckman, "We can't throw the son-of-a-bitch out. I ain't even got my jock wet . . . but you gotta handle McGuire. Let the Technicals and Sloan stay. Now get over the other side of the court. You hug that South Carolina sideline and don't come over here for anything! Period!"

When Grossman got over to the South Carolina side, McGuire called him over. The nattily dressed McGuire had this habit of pinching his tie knot up, screwing his head from left to right in his collar, and tipping his chin skyward before making a profound comment. This he did before saying to Grossman, "Hal, you threw him out!" Hal said to him, "Eckman tells me if I throw him out we'll never get out of this place alive." McGuire pinched his tie knot again, screwed his neck left to right, tipping his chin skyward and says, "Good call. We will go with the two 'Ts.' "

Chairish This

Eckman: "I was refereeing a play-off game with North Carolina in Raleigh. The game is tied and Dean Smith had put in a zone offense. With about one minute or so left to play, Larry Brown, the North Carolina guard, is on the outside holding the ball. I said to him, 'What time are we going to shoot this ball?' He said, 'I'll shoot with about ten seconds left, Mr. Eckman.' So I walked over to the Scorers' Table and I got a chair off the bench. I took the chair and set it mid-court. I said, 'Hell, if you ain't going to play, I ain't going to officiate.' I mean my legs hurt anyhow. So, I got a chair and pulled it out and sat right at mid-court and the place went wild. Dick Herbert, who was writing for the Raleigh paper in those days, a great basketball writer, was dying laughing. Everybody was taking pictures. It was on TV all over the country.

"I sat there and said, 'When you are ready, let me know!' He said, 'OK, We're ready.' I put the chair back and refereed. I don't remember who won or lost and I could care less. I had to do something to shake them up. From that time on the ACC changed the rules and put in the 30-second rule for the next season.

"Before the rule was changed, North Carolina Coach Dean Smith put in the four-corners offense. Believe me, the Tarheels could kill a clock passin' and passin' the ball around. I was happy to see them kill time off that game clock. It didn't matter to me. I got the same money, no matter who won or what happened. You just had to stay out there 40 minutes . . . and I had a lot of fun."

According to Hal Grossman, Dean Smith had such respect for Charley's officiating that when Charley was assigned, he would tell his players not to give the refereeing crew a hard time. Let them officiate because they knew what they were doing.

The Power of Green

One ACC game gave Eckman one of his most memorable moments. It was during the "Jim Crow" era.

Eckman: "I was officiating when 'Jumping' Johnny Green became the first black player to play in the South. I'm refereeing the Dixie Classic in Raleigh, North Carolina. The Michigan State University comes down and they've got Green on the team.

"Green comes on to the court and you can hear all the fans in the stands mumbling and muttering racial epithets. Green is the Center and he looks really nervous when he comes out for the opening tip-off. I am ready to throw the ball up and I look at Green and I said, 'Relax, nothing is going to happen out here.' He says, 'Thanks, ref.'

"Green gets the tap and the game is on. Then Bing! Bop! Bop! . . . about three or four minutes into the game, the ball hits the backboard with four players around the hoop and Green explodes up in the air. He gets that ball and comes down with it. You could hear the crowd go, 'Ooooh,' and 'Aaaah!' That's after they had been calling him all kind of vile names. And this is a college crowd, not a bunch of yo-yo's.

"Every time he would soar through the air and get a rebound, the crowd would gasp. By the time the game was over, he was one of the boys from down South. This Green had turned white and made believers of everyone at that game.

"He played pro ball with the Baltimore Bullets and he was a great rebounder. Jumping Johnny was a real class guy and I liked him."

The Real Power in the South

Eckman: " 'Footsie' Knight was a big man down South because he gave out the refereeing assignments. He lived in Durham and he was a physical training instructor. My friend

Louie Eisenstein, from New York, wanted to referee games in the South. Now, there is a lot of politics played in refereeing. One year, Louie sent 'Footsie' Knight's two grandsons little Duke uniforms. Louie had the uniforms made up in Brooklyn, New York, complete with numbers and the kids' names on them. You think he wasn't trying to get games?"

Down Memory Lane

Referee Louie Bello, who could best be described as an eccentric, was another Eckman officiating partner. During a game on the University of Maryland court, he didn't blow a whistle. After a spectacular foul call by Charley, Bello ran over to him, picked him straight up by the waist and carried him around the court shouting, "Eckman! You're the Greatest! Eckman! You're the Greatest!"

Two players get into a scuffle, more of a shove-and-push dance than a real fight, Eckman comes flying through the crowd and hollers, "Technical, technical on both of you. You can't play (*basketball*) and you can't fight. You're out of here!"

NEA Sports Writer Sandy Padwe reported on March 10, 1967: "Charley was always at the foul line with that big grin, and he always was around with the quick retort to any player who started to gripe . . . And always the sense of humor.

"Once an exhausted South Carolina player collapsed at Charley's feet after a fast break. 'Tired?' Charley asked. 'Cholly, I'm beat,' the youngster replied.

" 'Well, you just lay there awhile,' Charley said, the grin splitting his face. 'I got the ball and you got to throw it in to start play so nobody's going anywhere without us.' "

Eckman even received fan mail from coaches.

In February of 1962, University of South Carolina basketball coach Bob Stevens sent this note to Charley.

"Just a short note to express my sincere appreciation for the fine job you have done in handling our basketball games which you have officiated. This is not confined to just the Clemson game, of which 1 thought you did an excellent job and had very little help; but also to the Tennessee game, the Duke game, the Furman game, and certainly an outstanding job in the Clemson game.

L to R: Eckman, Burl Ives, ACC Official, and Hal Grossman at 1966 ACC Tournament. Ives became a big Eckman fan.

"Keep up the good work and in speaking in the behalf of the team, I hope that we will have an opportunity to have you work many of our games in the future."

A veteran Maryland sports columnist, Harry S. Russell, reported that the veteran Mr. Eckman was once a rookie, too: "They tell of a time when he was just breaking into college officiating and was sent to work a game in nearby Pennsylvania. He didn't know the older official who was to share the refereeing so he asked: 'Do you want me to work this side and this end and you the other?' The reply was: 'Son, I'll blow the whistle. You just fetch the loose balls.'"

The Really Big Show

Eckman: "The last time I refereed in the NCAA finals was the year Ohio State got upset by Cincinnati down in Louisville, Kentucky. Ohio State was loaded. They had Jerry Lucas and John Havlicek and that bunch. Bobby Knight, the Indiana coach, was the sixth man off the bench. Cincinnati didn't have any big names on their team. It was a kind of a game that Ohio

State fellows were suppose to win by a lot of points. I always found Bobby Knight to be a sharp guy, a good coach. He used to be a player/coach in the Army.

"Any how, I refereed that game and Cincinnati upset Ohio State and that's the last time I worked the NCAA finals. I would be selected by the Atlantic Coast Conference, go to Philadelphia, then go to Iowa City or some place out in the Midwest. And then the finals would come and I would come back East and stay."

You can't travel those many miles, for those many years, and referee in those many games without forming opinions on people, places and things.

Chapter

12

Full Court Press

One of the questions to be answered in the original Sports edition of the popular game Trivial Pursuit *asked who is the only person to officiate and coach in the NBA All-Star Game? You know the answer but here are questions that did not make the game.*

Who was the luckiest coach in the NBA?

What NBA Official was known as "The Mogul?"

What great NBA player learned to shoot with his left hand when his right arm was broken?

Name the New York night spot that was the basketball hangout in the '50s and 60s?

Name the best East teams in the early days of the NBA league?

The Luck of the 'Red' Irish

Eckman: "Red Auerbach, the coach of the Celtics, was the luckiest man that ever walked on this earth 'cause he didn't want no part of Bob Cousy or Bill Russell when he got them.

"He got "stuck" with Bob Cousy. The NBA had a dispersal draft when the Chicago Stags disbanded. They had a drawing and Red wanted Andy Phillip to be his playmaking guard, or Max Zaslofsky 'cause Zas could score. He wound up getting Cousy, which proves it's better to be lucky than to be good.

"Cousy made the Celtics run. He was a great passer . . . he had great peripheral vision and he could hit the open man. But, we beat Boston every time until they got Russell.

"Auerbach didn't want Bill Russell either. He got Russell from St. Louis owner Ben Kerner. The Celtics traded Cliff Hagen and somebody else for Russell. Kerner didn't know what he had drafted. Had Kerner kept Bill Russell, Kerner would have been the top man in pro basketball. Bill Russell was the human eraser. When he got in the League, he changed the whole style of play. Russell made the Celtics.

"Bill Russell had the greatest reflexes of anybody I ever saw. He would give Larry Foust fits. I remember the first night we played in Boston with Russell in the line-up. I didn't know Russell other than what I was told about him from a former pro player, "Apples" Kudelka.

"Well, we go against Russell and the Celtics and I tell Larry Foust to hit him to see if he has any guts . . . throw an elbow into him. Foust is about 6'9," a big strong guy. Foust backed up and he banged Russell a shot in the gut and he'd bang him a second time. Larry took that jumper of his and Russell got on top, and swat! . . . he hit Foust on the top of the head with the ball.

"Foust came away from that basket mumbling and shaking his head. The next time he comes by the bench, he asks me what to do. I said, 'Hit him again! The son of a bitch ain't that good.' OK, he says and he goes back in the pivot a second time. We throw the ball into Foust. My team clears the side. Foust is working on Russell. He takes his jumper and Russell got on top and hit the ball down on his head again . . . hard!

"The name of NBA Commissioner Maurice Podoloff was written on all the NBA basketballs. When Foust went by the bench I saw that he had 'Podoloff' etched on his forehead.

"Foust hollers to me, 'Stick that play up your ass!' I said, 'You're right! Forget it. He's too good for us.' Russell made a believer out of everybody. He was the reason the Celtics won.

"Before Russell, the Celtics had "Easy Ed" Macauley, who was a former St. Louis Bomber. Macauley was a good player. He wasn't a natural center. He was a hell of a shooter for a big man 6'7" or 8". He could shoot his little soft jumper outside the top of the key. But he wasn't strong enough to play the pivot, and everybody in the league knew it. The other teams would take him in there. But McCauley left the Celtics and here comes Russell. One player can make or break you.

"Defensive players mean so much, especially in today's game where you play offense all the time. You look at this guy Olajuwan, down in Houston. He is a defense ball player, and he is becoming an offensive player. His greatest assets are his reflexes and timing. The same way with Patrick Ewing, of the Knicks. At Georgetown, Ewing was more of an offensive player than Olajuwan. The defense will win more games for you than the offense. The defense keeps you in the game until the other guys make a mistake or two and you beat them. That's what happens when you play good defense. You can beat the opposition."

There were more than Knicks in New York

Two of the outstanding teams in the early days of the NBA were in upstate New York. In addition to respecting the team players, Charley liked the owners and coaches. Sometimes, one and the same.

Rochester's Royals

Eckman: "The Rochester Royals were a great ball club. They had Bobby Wanzer and Bobby Davies on the outside. Big Arnie Risen, Jack Coleman from Louisville, and Artie Johnson were the upfront guys. Wanzer and Davies were the same type of guard . . . drive and shoot. Wanzer was a better set shot but, Davies could drive better. Davies had no class.

"Wanzer, who went to Seton Hall, was a good guy . . . a lot of fun. We called him "Hooks." He would shoot through the skylight and he kept that Rochester team together. Davies was very upset because he didn't get the Fort Wayne Pistons coach job. He didn't know that Zollner hated his guts.

"Rochester had a great coach named Lester Harrison. Lester owned the team and he had his brother Jack out in front of the Edgerton Park Arena selling tickets, or so they tell me. I don't know if Jack was scalping the tickets or not. But in those days, Edgerton Park Arena was packed every night.

"Another good guy was Coleman. The big men, Risen and Johnson could shoot and rebound.

"It was great to watch Vern Mikkelsen, big, strong Swede

with the Lakers go at it with the Royals' Artie Johnson, another big Swede. They would get together on the floor in Rochester and they would lean against one another. They would hold one another up. I would run by and say, 'How do you feel, fellows?' And they would say fine Charley, don't bother us, we are all right. Go referee somewhere else . . . blow the whistle somewhere else. Those guys never bothered anybody. They didn't fight anybody.

"In Rochester, the backboards were slanted and the balls must have had some air taken out of them because every time Arnie Risen took a hook shot, the ball would hit the top of the backboard and come right on down through the hoop. I mean, that baby died on the backboard.

"A lot of teams tried to create an edge at their home courts. If you didn't rebound well but you blocked out well, your side would just take a little bit of air out of the ball. The ball would come down closer to the backboard.

"If your team was strong and could rebound well, your team would pump up the ball with a little more air. That way it would come off of that backboard and hit that rim and you would get the tip and push it out to the Guards on the outside. The referees didn't have any gauges . . . who the hell had a gauge? We were lucky to get a ball to get the game started. Throw the ball up in the air and if it bounces . . . let's play. Today, it is a little different. Referees today get more money. They use three referees in a game. We were lucky to have two. Many times in the old BAA, I would be refereeing the games by myself in places like Waterloo, Sheboygan, Iowa or in Denver or in Moline when nobody else showed up to referee with me.

"Rochester was a good town to referee in because the court was so compact you had to stay on the outside of the action. When you go inside, there was a lot of contact. When the Royals were hitting, nobody beat them."

The Boys From Syracuse

Eckman: "Danny Biasone, one of the finest owners in the game, had the Syracuse Nationals. He was a little Italian guy who ran a bowling alley up in Syracuse. He lived out of his pockets but he was a class guy. Al Cervi ran the ball club. He was in the service with me as a physical training instructor during World War

II. Cervi was the digger . . . he was a driver . . . a hard nose fellow. He played good defense and he knew how to play the whole game.

"Dolph Schayes of the Syracuse Nationals was without a doubt one of the best competitors I have ever seen. I refereed the playoffs between Syracuse and the great Minneapolis Lakers in 1954. We went to seven games. Schayes was playing with a broken arm and he did a tremendous job. Believe me, Schayes was unreal at times. When he broke his right arm, he learned to shoot with his left. Schayes was about 6'6" or 6'7" . . . he had a two-hand set and he could drive to the basket. He wanted to play all the time. He was an absolutely great ball player in his day, but he could play in today's game . . . no two ways about it!

"Paul Seymour was a fine guard . . . knew how to handle the ball . . . knew how to run the club if Cervi wasn't in the game. They were pretty much the same type of players. And then you had Wally Osterkorn who was the hitter . . . a good fellow . . . a great rebounder, not much of a shooter, but a tremendous guy. 'Bullet' Billy Gabor would drive on you. They beat me in the playoffs one year in seven games. They shouldn't have. We should have won that one.

"Syracuse had wild fans. They were all the rowdies up there and they got away with a lot of stuff in Syracuse that you wouldn't get away with in other towns. I'll never forget the guy they called 'The Strangler' who grabbed me as I was coming off the floor."

And then there were the Knickerbockers

Madison Square Garden was the home of the New York Knicks. According to Eckman, the Knicks were a good club to referee.

Eckman: "Carl Braun could shoot. He had this jumper . . . a one-hand push shot. Braun was most likely the best shooter on the club and a real class guy . . . a good looking guy. Ernie Vandeweghe was an excellent player. He went out to be a Hollywood physician . . . a great fellow . . . a good competitor. His college team was Colgate. Also on the team were Ray Lumpp and Harry 'The Horse' Gallatin. 'The Horse' didn't have that much ability, but he was aggressive and had good timing . . . he was a competitor. Gallatin could get rebounds that guys 7' tall couldn't get. He was only 6'5" or 6". He'd get the ball because of his positioning. The New York Knicks were a running ball club. The coach of the Knicks at that time was Joe Lapchick. He was a fine fellow, a good coach and a solid guy. He liked to call his players his 'kids' all the time."

The Hangouts

New York held charms for Charley that weren't on the basketball court, but where the fans would gather. In other words, New York had a lot of great hang outs.

Among Eckman's favorite eateries was *Mama Leone's* where Billy Sullivan and old Gene Leone rolled out the red carpet for Eckman and other basketball officials. Another of Charley's favorite persons was Lou Walters, who owned *The Latin Quarter*, and the father of Barbara Walters of TV fame. *Toots Shor's* place was a baseball hangout where Joe DiMaggio and Milton Berle were frequent visitors, and Eckman on occasion.

Charley used to stay at the Manhattan Hotel right across the street from *Jim Downey's* establishment on Eighth Avenue. The theater gang from Broadway would hang in *Downey's*.

Eckman's favorite spot was *Gilhooley's*. The Irish and Italian cops would all be in Joe Gilhooley's. The priests would come to the NITs with their colleges and Charley believed that ninety percent of them would go down to Joe Gilhooley's to celebrate and have fun.

> Eckman: "Joe, who went to Fordham, would tell stories about how he carried a machine gun when he was a bootlegger and how he'd run booze across the bay. We would all be there listening to him tell some cockamamie stories. Joe would lock up the joint so the priests could relax and have a few drinks by themselves. We would have a ball. There was a guy named Sullivan out of Syracuse who ran a beer distributorship. He came down every year and he treated everybody. Edward Everett Horton, the movie actor, used to come in a lot and so did the West Pointers. It was a great meeting place for people and it was like an old Irish saloon.
>
> "That's when Eighth Avenue was Eighth Avenue. With all the cops in *Gilhooley's*, we didn't have any trouble in those days. Today, New York is called Fort Apache. I loved the Garden and I liked New York in my time. I wouldn't go to New York now unless I had a hand-grenade."

The Philadelphia Story: Eckman's Version

If the Atlantic Coast Conference was the best conference Eckman ever officiated in, then Philadelphia was the best city for collegiate basketball.

Eckman: "Philadelphia was a great basketball town. They had that Big Five basketball colleges in Philadelphia. I used to referee on Friday night in college ball . . . and Philly had the greatest college basketball in the United States of America at that time. They had great teams like Villanova, St. Joe, LaSalle, Temple and Pennsylvania."

A Tribute to "The Mogul" and Others

Eckman: "Philadelphia had a lot of colorful people. One of the best was Eddie Gottlieb who kept the NBA running. He had the whole NBA schedule on his sleeve. Gottlieb, without a doubt, was the reason the NBA is alive today and cookin'. Every man who was ever involved with the NBA should thank his stars for Eddie Gottlieb. Eddie was the most intelligent man I have ever met in basketball. They use to call him 'The Mogul.' He was the finest. Eddie was also the owner of the Warriors. When the game would start he would be dressed. By the time the first half was over, he was half undressed . . . coat off . . . shirt off . . . Anything he could take off, he would take off.

"Joe Fulks, who played for the Warriors, is one of the most colorful persons of all time. You talk about shoot . . . Fulks could shoot the eyes out of the hoop. Regardless of how he was feeling, good or bad, he had that one-hand jumper he could score with. He could drive . . . he could rebound.

"Tommy Gola came out of LaSalle, played with the Warriors. He helped beat me in the playoffs one year. Gola was a great athlete at 6'5" or 6'6". He could jump and he could run. He was maybe the outstanding college basketball player in that era.

"Philly had a guy named Chuck Halbert on the team. He was a big cry baby from Texas. All he did was moan . . . every play was a foul. Every time he went down on the floor, you had to hear it. Off the floor he wasn't a bad guy, but on that floor he cried all the time. Another of the good guys was 'Chink' Crossin, who became a referee later on.

"George Senesky, the coach, was a real serious kind of a guy, but a real good guy . . . quiet. George was always thinking. He was ahead of his time in his pro basketball coaching thinking."

As for Charley's Who's Who . . .

Who's Who—NBA Leaders

Eckman: "**Maurice Podoloff** was the commissioner of the NBA. He had been the owner of a hockey team in New Haven, Connecticut. He was a great guy . . . a little fellow about five foot tall and he was a smart man, a lawyer, and he did a lot of good things for pro basketball. He got all the team owners together. That was a tough job considering all the egos involved.

"**Fred Zollner** was a very wealthy man. He owned a piston factory in Fort Wayne which supplied the pistons to General Motors among other major companies. He kept the NBA alive when Podoloff was the commissioner of the league. A lot of the team owners used to live from hand to mouth. Zollner would lend money to them and he helped to support the League. In fact, he kept the NBA alive after Podoloff died.

"**David Stern**, the future NBA Commissioner: 'I'm in New York to referee the game between the Sheboygan Redskins and the New York Knicks in the late '40s. I'm walking down Eighth Avenue behind a young kid walking with his father. The kid says to his dad, 'Gee, Dad, the Indians are going to play the Knickerbockers tonight.' His father says, 'No, son. The team is the Sheboygan Redskins.' The kid didn't know the difference. He learned fast. Now he's the commissioner who saved the NBA."

Eckman on Camp Followers

Eckman: "Now, let me tell you . . . those people who go to these camps to learn how to referee and how to umpire . . . well that's a joke. If you know the sport and you can express yourself and you're good at showmanship . . . have some guts and common sense . . . know the rules and have good judgment and a big voice, then you can referee. The idea is to get along with the ball players and the hell with the coaches.

"If you get along with the ballplayers up front, you would have no problem. Coaches give you the same stuff all the time looking for an edge. That didn't bother me. I would talk to the coaches in their native tongue and I didn't have any problem.

"You have to know the rules . . . and, I knew the rules. When you have rules, they are made to be broken. You interpret the rules as you want. Ya' tell 'em 'That's not the way I saw it!' . . . and you tell them the way you saw it. The hell with the rules!"

Eckman on College Coaches

Eckman: "**Honey Russell**, the Seton Hall coach, was one of the best. He knew how to handle men and he was a super guy. I later worked for him as a baseball scout when he was with the Milwaukee Braves.

"**Ben Carnevale**, who was down at the Naval Academy, got more out of less personnel than anybody I ever met. The Navy had height rules in those days and his tallest players were a few inches over six feet. Carnevale had his club in excellent shape. The teams at Navy and West Point were always in good shape.

"**Bobby Knight**, Indiana coach, does an excellent job I think. He was a smart player, an intense coach and a hell of a recruiter. Despite all his publicized scraps, he's a good guy.

"**Dean Smith**, North Carolina, is an excellent coach. He coaches defense. At North Carolina, Smith installed the four-corner offense . . . that's defense. They hold the ball . . . they pass the ball into the corner until they can get a good shot or the time on the clock runs out. Dean Smith is without a doubt the top coach in the country because he teaches good defense and that's what his offense is . . . defense! His team holds the ball. Hard as hell to shoot the ball when the other guy has got it.

"**Joe Lapchick** coached St. John's in New York. He was a great coach, but he was a better college coach than he was a pro coach.

"**Frank McGuire**, coached at both St. John's and South Carolina, was a great recruiter. If you can recruit well, you can become a pretty good college coach. If you can't recruit, you might as well write home for money.

"**Everett Case** was a terrific recruiter when he was coaching North Carolina State. Ev would primarily recruit in Indiana. He was also a super guy who looked out for his players.

"**Rollie Massamino** had his troubles after moving from Villanova to UNLV, in Las Vegas, Nevada. He moved into a tough situation because of the recruiting scandal at Nevada plus his contract. Massamino didn't kill anybody out there with his great skills because he can't recruit like Tark, The Shark, his predecessor. It's as simple as that. Rollie was the assistant coach for Doggie Julian at Dartmouth when I refereed.

"**Doggie Julian** used to get his teams at Dartmouth all stirred up. He was a holler guy. I don't think he had any set plays. He just went out and had a good time and his players did too. Doggie loved the horses and I used to see him at the race track often.

"**Fuzzy Levane** was the coach of the Milwaukee team that later went to St. Louis. They were a very ordinary team and the Lakers were the champs. Milwaukee beats the Lakers one night in an exhibition game in a tiny little town in Wisconsin. Fuzzy, who stuttered when he got excited, was on the phone in the hotel lobby, calling the Milwaukee Journal newspaper. He is describing how *his team* beat the Lakers by one point! Now, we can hear what's happening in the lobby. The guy from the newspaper is saying something like what's so important about beating the Lakers in an exhibition? Fuzzy is hollering, 'What do you think this is, chopped beef?! We beat the Lakers! We ain't beat the Lakers in two years! What's the matter with you!' Fuzzy was a good guy . . . a good ball player . . . and he was quite a person."

Eckman's capsule comments on the players who rated in the early days of the National Basketball Association.

Eckman: "**Paul Arizin** was a great jump shooter, a real competitor and strong kid who could do a lot of things well. He was much stronger than he looks.

"**Elgin Baylor** was a great college player and he could play on any team, any time. He was the first player I ever saw hang in the air. He did the Michael Jordan thing and he did it before Jordan was ever born. Elgin Baylor could go to the top of the key and fly to the hoop without taking a step. Believe me, he could hang. Elgin just came along in the wrong era to make the big money.

"**Ralph Beard**, with Indianapolis, was without a doubt the best all around guard in pro basketball. He could have played in any era. Beard could run like a deer, shoot the ball and score.

He was always chewing gum . . . a clean-cut nice guy. It was a terrible thing when he got caught in the point-shaving scandals. It really hurt me because I thought Beard was going to be the best ball player of his time.

"**Carl Braun**, with New York, was the best the Knicks had. He was their 'go to guy' before that phrase became a cliché.

"**Bob Cousy**, with Boston, was without a doubt the best passer I ever saw. He knew what he was doing at all times . . . the 'Flying Frenchman.' He wasn't that good of a shooter but certainly he could make the fast break go. Cousy would be the kind of a guy you want on your club if your team could run.

"**Bobby Davies**, with Rochester, could drive and shoot with anybody, but he had a terrible attitude.

"**Tom Gola**, with Philadelphia, was an outstanding college basketball player at LaSalle. Gola could do it all. Gola would have played in any era any time. He could play today, tomorrow or next year.

"**Mel Hutchins**, with the Pistons—I said it before and I'm saying it again. Mel was the greatest defensive player in the country until Bill Russell came along to change the game. Hutchins could jump out of the building. He made the Pistons a winner when I coached there with his defense. Oddly enough, he didn't really love to play the game.

"**George Mikan**, with the Minnesota Lakers, could turn around and make that little shot. He was 6'11" and strong as a bull. He would just dump the ball in the basket. Any opposition player trying to defend against him would just go in with it. He was the first pro basketball superstar, but I think he would be just another player in today's game.

" '**Easy' Ed Macauley**, with St. Louis, was a natural forward who often played center because of his height. He had this little soft push shot and he could score.

"**Al McGuire** played for St. John's in college and the Knicks in the pros. He was not the player his brother Dick was. He was a hatchet man, an enforcer. He would jump around and nail guys, but he was a good guy and who would do anything in the world for you if he knew you. On the court, he was the kind of guy who was always in foul trouble and he knew he was going to be. His job was to excite the people . . . get the spectators up and keep the opposition honest.

"**Dick McGuire**, with the New York Knicks, was a top notch ball handler and field general but he didn't shoot much. Late in his career, I got him at Detroit.

"**Jim Pollard**, with the Minnesota Lakers, was without a doubt one of the all time basketball greats. He could jump, play defense, and he fed the ball to George Mikan so that the big man could score. Jim was a great passer.

"**Bob Pettit**, with St. Louis, could play in any era. As far as I am concerned, Bob Pettit was as smart a ball player as I have ever seen.

"**Andy Phillip**, with the Pistons, was a great ball handling quarterback. Unlike McGuire, Phillip could shoot. He, Cousy, and Dick McGuire, were the best ball handling guards. All were great guys too.

"**George Yardley**, with the Pistons, really had the competitive spirit and he could shoot too. He was a great basketball player, a pure shooter. He had a slight build but he was another guy who could jump like a kangaroo.

"**Bobby Wanzer**, with Rochester, was not as good a shooter as Davies, but he was a better ball player and a lot nicer person.

"**Jerry West**, with Los Angeles, I think was the best college basketball player. He played at the University of West Virginia, for Freddie Schaus. Freddie was a pretty good pro player in his own right. West could do it all as a college basketball player. He had a great attitude . . . he could rebound and then lead the fast break. He changed a great deal when he went to the pros. It all went to his head.

"**Johnny Nucatola** was the head referee for a time in the NBA. He officiated a little bit in the pro's, but he was not a pro-type referee. He was too much like a school marm. He was a school teacher."

The BAA Bunch

These are some of the players that started their professional careers in the old Basketball Association of America, and may have not gotten the recognition they deserved in the NBA.

Eckman: "**Mike Todorovich** was a great player for the Moline team. He had a lot of ability, but he played for the wrong team. When you play with the wrong team, no matter how good you are, you are never going to get the recognition that you deserve. Of course, if you didn't play around the New York area, you didn't get recognition either.

"**Leo Barnhorst** was also with Moline in the Mid-West. He had a good two-hand set.

"**Bob Feerick** played for the Washington Caps. He was an excellent ball player and a big shooter from outside. He had a one-hand set shot.

"**Bruce Hale** may have been the best looking basketball player ever. A real Hollywood type. He played with the Indianapolis Kautskys, named after the team owner, in the old BAA, and later with the Indianapolis Olympians. He was a fancy ball

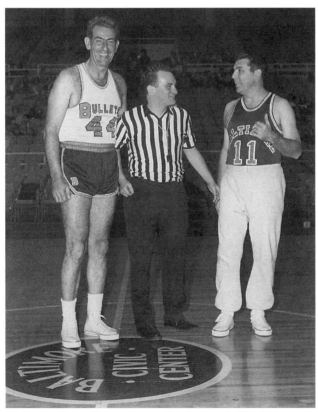

Eckman officiated at numerous charity events. This 1960 game at the Baltimore Civic Center featured Bullet favorites Mike Bloom (L) and Basketball Hall of Famer Buddy Jeannette (R).

handler. He later became the father-in-law of Rick Barry, who was terrific shooter at the University of Miami and also played in the pros.

"**Buddy Jeannette** was the player/coach of the old Baltimore Bullets. The Bullets won a BAA Championship under Jeanette. The amazing thing about Jeanette was that he could drive but he couldn't see the basket. He would get fouled a lot and make the foul shots.

"**Paul 'The Bear' Hoffman** didn't get his nickname from runnin' around the court naked. For a guy about 6'3", he was a tough rebounder and competitor. He was an enforcer type. The funny thing was that he won the Rookie of the Year award in 1948 in the BAA, but the NBA didn't recognize it until 1994.

"**Herman Schaefer** played with the old Lakers in the BAA. He was a real good guard in the wrong era. He could do a lot of things with the ball and had a good two-hand set shot.

"**Freddy Scolari**, with the Washington Caps, had a one-hand push shot from his belly. Freddy could hit that shot without even looking at the basket. It was like he was drawing a gun and shooting from the waist in a wild west movie. He was very competitive."

Way Out West

Eckman: "The Phoenix Webbcos, owned by New York Yankee owner Del Webb, had Chet McNabb, a forward, and Ralph Basket, a guard, who never got a chance to play in the pro ranks because they played out in the West where nobody could see them. They were legitimate big-time players who could have made it in the pro leagues.

"Another standout was Scotty Hamilton, who came from the great state of West Virginia. Scotty played for the San Diego Dons in the industrial league. He was a guard and a real tough guy. He is another one who should have been a pro but who went undiscovered."

An Eckman Trip Down Memory Lane

"**Havlicek versus McGill:** John 'Hondo' Havlicek was a tremendous ballplayer, underrated. I recommended him to the St. Louis Hawks owner Ben Kerner. Kerner drafted Bill 'The

Hill' McGill instead. McGill was about 6'11" and he had a little turn-around shot. Havlicek could do it all. He could run all night, the 'Hondo Kid.' 'The Hill' turned out to be a mole hill and 'Hondo' became an All Pro and he saved the Boston Celtics after Russell was gone.

"**Frank Robinson**, Baseball Hall of Famer, former baseball manager and current baseball executive. Freddie Scolari and 'Apples' Kudelka, two former pro players, told me that when I go to San Francisco, I should watch a kid by the name of Frank Robinson. If Frank would have gone to college, I would have drafted him for the Pistons. He was a hell of a basketball player and team leader, but he chose baseball and did pretty good.

"**The Bevo Bust**: The most overrated big man I ever saw was a guy from a little town in Ohio. His name was Bevo Francis, from Rio Grande, Ohio. His college publicity man may have stretched him to 6'7". His college got a lot of publicity as Bevo's team beat a lot of bad teams. Bevo must have been 28 or 29 years old when he played against North Carolina State down at Raleigh. He helped to pack the house wherever he played because he scored 35, 45, 50 points a game. He was an ordinary ballplayer at his best. His coach was smart, very smart, because the team earned a lot of money and that might have saved the Rio Grande School.

"**The Los Angeles Red Devils**: The Devils were a barnstorming basketball team that carried just six players. They were all baseball players who would get together after the season and play all over the Far West, from Phoenix to Los Angeles. Big George Crowe, a first baseman for the St. Louis Cardinals, was the center. Irv Noren, an outfielder for the Chicago Cubs, was a forward. A young kid who was in his first year of baseball with Montreal was the guard. He was a legitimate basketball player who could have played pro basketball—but Jackie Robinson was destined for baseball history."

Eckman on the Harlem Globetrotters

Eckman: "The original Harlem Globetrotters really didn't play basketball. It was just showtime that's all, but what a show! They just put the show on and people liked it. 'Goose' Tatum was 6'3". He had big hands but he couldn't do nothing but showboat.

They had a couple of good players on the club. Not many people will remember that Bob Gibson, the fire-balling pitcher for the St. Louis Cardinals, played for the Globetrotters one year. Marques Haynes could really dribble and handle the ball. Babe Pressley was pretty good, but the Globetrotters didn't have any great basketball players. They had a lot of good guys who could put on a hell of a show. There were times I would referee a Globetrotters game in the first half of a double header, and an NBA game in the second. I put on a show in both halves of the double header."

The Experiment

Eckman was part of a noble experiment in the old BAA. One of the league officials came up with the bright idea to try officiating from the tennis standpoint . . . or sit point. Why not have one referee, like they do in tennis, sit in a high chair on the side of center court. Ball boys, like in tennis, would retrieve errant basketballs and bring them back to restart play.

The old coliseum on Monroe Street in Baltimore was picked as the site of experiment and Charley was selected to be the officiating "experimentee".

Eckman: "For three quarters, everything went fine. I sat there on that high chair and I went, 'Toot, toot! You! Foul. Take two . . . Toot! Foul! Take the ball out of bounds . . . these ball boys are running around and grabbin' the balls that went out of bounds, and bringing them back to court. Toot, toot! . . . the end of the third quarter.

"Now, anybody who has seen me referee, knows that I'm demonstrative . . . and being up in that chair, I had to be . . . careful. But, I'm really into the game. Toot! Hacking! Now, I'm standing up on the rung of this high chair showing the hacking . . . and now I'm not standin' up any more . . . I'm diving head over teacups on to the court. Splat! End of experiment!"

Finally, Charley's legs blow the final whistle on his court career.

Chapter

13

The Legs are the
First to Know

" 'I'm a walking medical kit,' he said. 'I feel like a $2,000 dollar horse at Charles Town.' At 45, he claims to be escaping with only his sanity from the maddening arenas filled with 'screaming yo-yos.' . . . Now the savagery of the crowds has taken its toll. Once, a thrown beer can in Philadelphia's palestra broke his wrist . . .

"What Eckman loves to do is, as he says, 'give it the old federal case.' This involves a deliberate pause after' blowing his whistle until the crowd is quiet and anxiously turned toward him. He will emerge from the pack of players and bellow his decision, embellishing it with frantic arm and torso gestures and one final grand sweep with the right hand."
—*Syndicated Sports Writer William Gildea*

Southern Discomfort

Time was beginning to catch up with Charley. However, before that happened, Eckman, rated the best the year before, a man who refused to officiate games for certain teams, got the axe from the Southern Conference. His firing raised eyebrows and columns in the southern newspapers. One of the columns written by Jim Anderson headlined, "Eckman Sounds Warning."

"Charlie Eckman says he is 'an outspoken type of person.' Which is an understatement. Jolly Cholly is as outspoken, in rapid-fire style, as they come. Which could be just one reason he no longer is to officiate in Southern Conference basketball games.

"But the Glen Burnie, Md., native is not a man 'with a beef.' Rather, he conscientiously says he's 'fighting for what I think is right' when he attacks the method of coaches having the say-so on officials, as used by the Southern Conference.

"Eckman was released, dropped, fired by the conference after 25 years of officiating basketball games. Yesterday he told the Greenville Touchdown Club why. He put the finger on Coaches Lefty Driesell of Davidson and George King of West Virginia, with Bill Reinhart of George Washington as the 'kicker,' as the 'cuties who did the job on me.' And he told why he thought so.

"One warning sounded by Eckman was serious. He said intercollegiate sports would be ruined if only 'homers' officiated. 'That would be going back to the dark ages,' said Eckman. 'The Southern Conference has not given me one reason for being dropped,' said Eckman, who only last year was named the No. 1 college basketball official in the nation by an outstanding sports magazine . . .

"He thinks that the cessation with the Southern began at a George Washington-Maryland game, while calling it with Col. Joseph A. Barrett of Arlington, Va. . . . 'Maryland had the ball, and I was watching the 'cute stuff' underneath the basket. They (Maryland) took a shot. I have no idea if it's good or not. The buzzer sounded. Here they come!'

" 'I ask Barrett if it's good, or ain't good. All he's gotta say is one or the other. He forgot his name. He gave me that big blank look. I think, blankety, blank, we're in trouble. I go to the scorer's table. The scorer's table is the last place in the world you want to go. He's from one school. He's gonna be there. Not down at VMI or Furman next week. He's got the monkey on his back . . . He says; 'Well, the ball was up there . . .'

" 'I shout, 'Goal's good, Maryland wins,' and walk away. Next year Barrett's out of the league and I'm black-balled.'

Eckman said he officiated in seven upset games last season.

" . . . One that was not an upset was Duke defeating West Virginia. But after that game Coach King of the Mountaineers told Eckman, 'I'm going to get you.' And Eckman added, 'He got me, all right.' But Charlie said WVU couldn't have beaten Duke with three teams.

"The upsets included games such as 'the Richmonds beating the Citadels, and Richmond couldn't beat Molly Clutchs' Athletic Club.' But he's told after the game what a great job he did.

"Then he has 'the Davidsons and VMIs' in the conference tournament. Davidson has to win to draw the crowds, pointed out Eckman, because VMI 'doesn't have seven alumni between here and Chicago.' But VMI wins and Eckman is told by Les Hooker, athletic director at W & M, 'Well, the white shirts won again tonight!' . . .

" 'I crucified myself in the Southern Conference,' continued Eckman, 'Because I've got guts . . .

" 'You're not out there to protect a team, but to work a ball game.' "

Years later, as a sportscaster, Charley evened the score with Lefty Driesell, who was then coach of the University of Maryland basketball team. When asked what he thought was wrong the Maryland team, Eckman said "Why aren't the Terps winning? Because of the dummy in charge. Lefty Driesell's got material coming out of his ears and he doesn't know what to do with it."

An Era Ends

His legs were shot, the years of abuse from the fans had taken its toll, and he had started a new career. Charley turned in his zebra stripes for good. His retirement produced a river of "ink."

Newsweek *reported his retirement in March 1967*: "They're turning the game into a joke,' complains basketball referee Charley Eckman. So what's funny about getting your upper plate knocked out by a thrown ball? Your wrist broken by a beer can? Other parts of your anatomy, pelted by peanuts, hot pennies and fish?

"After 29 years as a fast-moving target—and four twitchy seasons on the bench as a pro coach in the NBA—the battle-scarred Eckman stowed his whistle for keeps after last week's NCAA regionals in Evanston, Ill. But Eckman, 45, went out with a blast.

"Fans have seen a lot of action from the flamboyant Eckman himself. Often, when he calls a foul, he pumps his arm, kicks his leg and wrathfully races to the scorer's table.'

" 'Hold it!' he bellows. 'He's got a charge.'

"Eckman's histronics have made him unpopular with many fans and coaches, but his candor makes him a favorite with the players. In an Atlantic Coast Conference game, he made an admittedly bad call but explained to the victimized player: 'Look, kid, there's two seconds to play, and my feet hurt. I'm not walking 94 feet for a lousy free throw. The foul is on you.' Adds Eckman: 'You know, he agreed with me?'

"Guessing Game: Eckman regards foul calling as a guessing game at best. 'If we called fouls according to the book nobody would be left on the court after five minutes. The things that go on under the basket, I don't dare discuss . . . . '

"'There's no respect for law and order in the country,' he laments. 'If the cop on the beat can't arrest a guy and put him away, how do you expect somebody with a plastic whistle to run the show on the basketball court?' . . ."

NEA Sports Writer Sandy Padwe on March 10, 1967 wrote: "With the end of the collegiate basketball season also comes the end of Charley Eckman's career.

"Charley's career—a referee and as coach of the old Fort Wayne Pistons—has been colorful. It also has been controversial. It still is . . . .

" 'The rule book is the last thing to worry about. It is the poorest written book in the country.' It was Charley's 'feel for the game' that earned him the title, 'the player's referee.' And it is because Charley's lost this 'feel' that he has decided to retire.

" 'I've been in the game for 29 years,' he said. 'I'm 45. Why not go out on top? I'm not quitting because of anything the coaches or players pull. You can always keep them in line. It's the fans. They're getting worse. They're almost unbelievable.'

" 'I'm not talking about the guys in Madison Square Garden or the big arenas in the big cities. They're not really fans. They're gamblers. All they care about is the point spread. I'm talking about the kids on the campuses. Their behavior has been so bad that I'm inclined to believe games should be played on neutral courts.'

" 'Look, I don't mind the booing and all that. It's part of the game, part of the color and atmosphere. What I mind is the things they throw: beer cans, hot dogs, soda bottles, rolled-up programs, hot pennies . . .'

" 'The fans from Atlantic Coast and Southern Conference schools may not care about Charley's retirement, but the players will. He was their favorite."

United Press International on March 21, 1967 reported "Eckman Leaves 'Em Laughing: The ruddy-faced man run out from beneath the basket. 'Number 33, blue, you got him—and we're going that way!'

"Charlie Eckman points to the free throw line. The crowd laughs. He starts walking with a basketball under his arm toward the center of the court. Eckman, a Glen Burnie, Md. resident, has for years delighted Atlantic Coast Conference fans, coaches and other officials with his antics. Now, after 17 years calling games, he is retiring . . .

"Eckman's last game in the ACC was a meeting between South Carolina and Duke that had been billed as a grudge meeting because South

Carolina blames the Blue Devils for a conference ruling which declared highly-touted sophomore Mike Grosso ineligible.

"Relaxing in his room the day after the game, Eckman said 'That could have been a bad one. But it came off without a hitch. It sort of makes you feel like a hero.'

" 'Why, after the game, those South Carolina players came up to me and told me I called a good game. Every one of them did. That's really something when you consider they lost.'

"Although Eckman will not be calling games next season, he will still be active in sports. He has two sportscasts daily on a Baltimore station (WCBM) . . . He's also a popular after-dinner speaker in Pennsylvania, Maryland and other parts of the Atlantic seaboard.

"A typical Charlie Eckman game starts . . . bounces the ball from one sideline to the other before throwing up the tipoff. Then he goes into action, his gravel voice calling out the misdeeds of each side . . .

" 'It takes personality and poise. Most referees go out there looking for trouble, but the teams know I'm not going to hurt them. There have been some coaches who didn't like me, but never the boys,' he says."

There wasn't much he didn't know about the game. Basketball and Charley Eckman spoke the same language: "Put the ball in the basket and keep it simple because it's a very simple game."

Baltimore Columnist and TV Commentator Mike Olesker wrote:
" . . . There were the 29 seasons over which he refereed some 3,500 basketball games. He was beautiful to watch. He'd come roaring through forests of players, arms waving, body gyrating, whistle blaring, all action ceasing as Eckman bellowed to the rafters, 'Nobody move, I got this man throwing a hip.' "

William Gildea, the fine writer for the Washington Post, whose material frequently found its way into newspapers across the country, marked Charley's retirement as a referee.

"There is a touch of sadness about this basketball season. After 29 years and 3,500 games, Charley Eckman, the most colorful and, perhaps, best referee, is retiring. Not a few people are saddened because, uncharacteristic of referees, Eckman makes friends. The Maryland House of Delights (sic) passed a resolution citing his achievements.

"He won't be back, he insists, unless he needs the money. Basketball has gotten his last 'pound of flesh.' He has swollen ankles, which require icing; bursitis in his left shoulder, and a bad limp as a reminder of an operation on his right leg two years ago to remove a blood clot.

" 'I'm a walking medical kit,' he said. 'I feel like a $2,000 dollar horse at Charles Town.' At 45, he claims to be escaping with only his sanity from the maddening arenas filled with 'screaming yo-yos.' . . . Now the savagery of the crowds has taken its toll. Once, a thrown beer can in Philadelphia's Palestra broke his wrist . . .

"What Eckman loves to do is, as he says, 'give it the old federal case.' This involves a deliberate pause after blowing his whistle until the crowd is quiet and anxiously turned toward him. He will emerge from the pack of players and bellow his decision, embellishing it with frantic arm and torso gestures and one final grand sweep with the right hand . . . .

"A referee, Eckman says, must have 'poise, personality, and a pinch of psychology.' His cardinal rule is honesty, 'If I kick one I'll admit it to a coach. The idea is not to kick too many, particularly down the stretch in a tight game.

"'Refereeing is 90 per cent judgment and guts. Throw the rule book out or give it ten per cent at best. Most of all, you've got to have sense of humor in this racket. After all these years, that's all I've got.'"

Bill Tanton, the Evening Sun *Sports Editor put it this way:* "After 26 years of pounding his way up an down the nation's hardwoods—from Fourteen Holy Martyrs Hall to Madison Square Garden—Charley Eckman doesn't know how to act now that he's in drydock.

"Eckman, who grew up on Stricker street and has long since risen to the majestic position of unofficial mayor of Glen Burnie has been a 5-foot-8 giant in the game of basketball in recent years.

"He probably was the top referee in the game. His histrionics entertained crowds and players in the National Basketball Association and at top college games, including the National Invitational Tournament and the N.C.A.A. championships. In between, he coached the N.B.A. Pistons . . . This year he went back to officiating in the N.B.A., but after 30 games he pulled out.

" 'My legs were killing me early in the year," says Eckman. 'I've got a deterioration of the leg muscle and surgery couldn't correct it. But what finished me was the air travel. I never did like the planes, but this year it was murder. You're up there five hours on that flight to the Coast, they tell you you're going to encounter turbulence over the Grand Canyon at 37,000 feet. They might as well tell me I'm going to hell on a handcar.'"

Charley's retirement from basketball left a void for one ACC fan who wrote to Jack Horner of the Durham *Morning Herald*:

"Dear Jack,

"While there can be no question that the officiating in the recent

Another charity game in the '60s, this one between the members of the Maryland House of Delegates and State Senate. Kneeling are Governor Marvin Mandel (on Charley's right) and WFBR News Director Lou Corbin (bottom right).

State-Duke game was atrocious, I think both you and Press Maravich are stating only half the facts . . .

" 'The officials, especially the ones in the ACC, seem to try to even up the calls, fouls or plain violations, and in doing so, really prejudice the good teams . . . I'll take Charley Eckman any old time. He seldom, if ever, lets a game get out of hand, and would not permit the starting of a Duke-State feud on his basketball court. If he had officiated the other night, you wouldn't have the small spark present to fan into something bigger.'"

Bill Brill, Basketball America *Executive Editor, and winner of the 1995 Jake Wade Award, presented annually by the college Sports Information Directors of America to a media member who has made a significant lifetime contribution to college sports, provided the ultimate insiders view of Charley in the August 1995 issue of Basketball* America. The article is entitled "Charlie Eckman, One Of Basketball's True Characters".

"In another time, pretelevision era, basketball referees were as big a part of the game as the coaches and players. Some, as incredulous as it may seem to youthful readers, may have had more fame.

"There was Red Mihalik, whose authority running a game was never questioned. Or Lenny Wirtz, who is still around nearly 40 years later, sitting on the Maryland bench during a timeout. Or Lou Bello, waiting for the proper moment to call a charge so that he could get on his horse and do a 'Hi-yo, Silver' dash to the other end of the floor. And even the less flamboyant, but nevertheless prominent, like the Mills brothers, Jim and Joe, who almost always worked together; Arnold Heft; Dr. Phil Fox; Lou Eisenstein.

"I can still recall their names more than a generation later, evidence that they were an integral part of a growing sport. Give yourself a quick test. See how many basketball officials you can name. Unless you are in the business, it will be in single figures. Today's prevailing theory is that officials are most effective when anonymous.

"But this was another time, in the '50s and '60s—Charlie Eckman's time.

"Charlie Eckman was the best official I ever saw. Not because he had the best judgment, or never missed one. But because he was in total command . . .

"I got to know Charlie after his stint as the Pistons coach . . . Years later, another Detroit coach would get fired and go on to greater fame in the game. Charlie never struck it big like Dick Vitale, but he was every bit as flamboyant.

"In those days, officials got paid little, so they begged, borrowed and scrimped, cutting corners at every opportunity. Over the years. I heard all the stories . . . Winning on the road was difficult, perhaps impossible, unless you got one of the precious few referees who were not beholden to their hosts.

"I recall a game in December, 1951, when Duke was playing at Bradley. When Blue Devil captain Dick Groat, later to be a longtime Pittsburgh Pirates shortstop, returned to the bench after the pregame meeting, he told coach Hal Bradley, 'I think we're in trouble.' "Squeaky" Melchiorre was the Bradley star, and after the introductions, one of the officials turned to him and said, 'Squeaky, where are we going after the game?'

Or the time that Virginia Tech and Wake Forest made a trip to play Toledo and Dayton, reversing opponents on opposite nights. Arriving in Dayton late at night, our group with Tech met Bones McKinney in the hotel lobby. Bones, the Wake Forest coach, told the Hokies' Chuck Noe, 'The zebras won't give you a chance.' The next morning's papers showed why. There was a picture of Bones, sitting in the end zone of the stands. He had been thrown out of the game on the opening play. But Bones always loved it when he saw Eckman come out on the floor, especially when the game was on the road.

"Charlie never stopped talking. He knew all the players and most of the sportswriters. He knew a lot of the fans. But no matter how much he smoozed, when the game was on, he was all business.

"In the winter of 1963, Duke took the nation's No. 1 team to Morgantown to play in West Virginia's Mountaineer Classic. The three visiting teams and all the officials stayed in the Morgan Hotel, not far from old Mountaineer Fieldhouse . . . On the day of the championship game between the Blue Devils and WV, a blizzard hit. The town was shut down.

"Eckman held fort in the lobby, talking basketball all day with the various players. In particular, he struck up a conversation with Duke star Jeff Mullens. When it came time to go to the game, there was no transportation for the officials. Without hesitation, Eckman boarded the Duke bus, the only thing that was moving.

"When WVU coach Fred Schaus found out that the referee had ridden to the game with the Duke team, he blew up. Eckman simply listened to the complaint. Early in the game, Mullens, the most mildmannered of players, made a comment after a foul call. Normally, it would have been overlooked by anybody, Eckman included.

"But Charlie whistled a technical foul on the startled Mullins. As he neared the scorer's table, he said, 'You may have been Jeff this afternoon, but you're only No. 44 tonight.' Eckman had made his point to Schaus. There was no danger that the officials had been influenced . . . "

For Eckman, the basketball court was a place of work. The Race Track was a place for fun . . . and sometimes . . . work.

Chapter

14

So This is How You
Improve the Breed—

Since being a basketball referee was a seasonal thing, and the need to make a living for his family was a year-round thing, Charley was always job hunting. He was friends with a ton of political figures including a number of Governors of Maryland including Governor Millard J. Tawes. Eckman campaigned for Tawes, whom he considered a great man.

At first Tawes offered him a job on the liquor board in Anne Arundel County, but Charley said no. Then, he appointed Eckman the Chief Judge of the Orphans Court in Anne Arundel County (but that's another story). Finally, the Governor named him a racetrack inspector.

An explicit description of a racetrack inspector is a, a . . . uh . . . urine retriever. The inspector walks behind the horse that wins the race . . . following winner from the paddock to the barn where it is stabled. The inspector had an assistant whose job it is to catch the urine specimen in a container. The urine is then sent to the lab to check on any illegal substance that could have enhanced the performance of the horse.

The "Honey's Tiger" Caper

Eckman: "Now, on this day out at Bowie, 'Honey's Tiger' won the second or third race of the afternoon. Tommy Lee rode him. So, we—me and my buddy (he's the guy with the jar) follow 'Honey's Tiger' back in the barn and the Hot Walker, one of the Back Stretch people, walked him around the shed row. The shed row is the area that surrounds the individual stables. The Hot Walker keeps walking him until the horse is ready to urinate. Every time it looks like 'Honey's Tiger' is getting ready, my buddy would run up and put the bucket where the horse would urinate.

"Well, 'Honey's Tiger' would have none of that. My assistant would move into position and the horse would back up. Now, we get some more Back Stretch people helping out . . . they put water on him . . . they take and mop and dusted him all in an effort to get 'Honey's Tiger' to urinate. The Groom, Hawkins, even tickles the horse to get him to piss. The horse ain't goin'.

"We're walking around with this horse since 1:30 in the afternoon and it is now 7 p.m. and it's dark. The Back Stretch people are all gone and I'm walking him up and down and around . . . I put him in the stall . . . pull him out . . . he makes out like he's going to go . . . he don't go . . . he pulls it back in.

"I said to my buddy, 'I think we have had enough . . . it's dark . . . everybody's gone but us. We've been here all day in this god damn barn. This horse don't want to do it.' He said, 'Christ, it's dark out here. It's getting late and we ought to get out of here.' I said, 'You are right . . . I've been here all day watching this horse drink water and walk around. He ain't about to urinate.' My buddy said, 'No, he ain't!' I said, 'Gimme that jug!' I took that jug and *I* became "Honey's Tiger" at 15 after 7 that night! It was dark as hell. That horse looked at me and he must have thought to himself something funny is going on. So, after I started urinating, the horse started pissing. The horse peed and I peed and we all became 'Honey's Tiger!' And that's how I finished up my career on the racetrack as an inspector."

In thoroughbred racing terminology an "Improver of the Breed" is a person who bets. I am not exactly certain how one who bets improves the breed of equine progeny, but the breeders of thoroughbred racehorses, owners of the horses and the racetracks, trainers, Hot Walkers and other important members of the Back Stretch family, mutual window operatives and thousands of others would be a sorry lot without the stiffs who bet.

For each dollar that is bet, a percentage goes to state and/or local government, the track owners and for purses paid to the owners of the winning entries, usually through the fourth-place finisher in the race.

Considering the contributions made to the racing industry via the mutual window, particularly in Maryland, Delaware, Pennsylvania, and West Virgina, Charles Markwood Eckman, Jr., is deserving of a place of honor in a Mid-Atlantic Horse Racing Hall of Fame, should one ever be built.

For Charley, horse racing started as a family affair. As a kid, seven or eight years old, he would go with his grandfather, a Baltimore and Ohio conductor, to Laurel Race Track where the B & O ran a train on racing days. In those days, betting was done through legitimate bookmakers outside the track. It was the bookies who set the odds on the different horses, often at odds with each other.

Charley's grandfather liked to bet, but not while he was in the B & O uniform. Charley would be his runner.

Eckman: "Grandpap would sit there and bet all day and I

Eckman (L) at Bowie Race track with Baltimore native Jack Portney.
Portney was Australian Welter-weight boxing champ and third ranked in U.S.

would run to the bookmaker with the money. One day, the old man won $28 and I had to go get the money from the bookmaker. My grandfather gave me a buck for running off the train and placing the bet. I said to myself, 'This is the game for me,' and I guess I've been around the races ever since."

Getting Religion at Laurel

Eckman took one of the favorite men of cloth in the Maryland sports world, Father Martin Schwalenberg, now a Monsignor, to Bowie Race Course, along with several members of the Fava family. The Favas are big in Baltimore in the fruit and produce business. Father Marty has been chaplain for the Baltimore Orioles. He was also chaplain for the old Baltimore Colts.

Eckman: "Father Schwalenberg came to the track just after blessing the house of air conditioning entreprenuer Vince Pipitone. I know this and I'm going to place a hunch bet on a horse called 'Bless This House.' Father Marty takes his collar off because he's going to make a wager.

"I tell him about 'Bless This House' because its a natural. He studies the racing form. Father Marty said, 'I can't bet that horse.' Johnny Fava agrees, 'No way can I bet this horse, either.' The horse is now at forty-five to one and the odds are going up. Its the first race and I said to myself, 'I've got to bet this horse.' I said to Father Marty, 'You just blessed the Pipitone's house, Marty and you aren't going with my hunch after all the praying you did today?'

"I bet ten dollars to win on the horse. 'Bless This House' wins and pays $95 and change for a $2 bet. Now, I look around for the Fava family, a very sincere solid Catholic family . . . and they are running away from me. I look around for Father Marty and he is crawling under the tables trying to get away from me and I'm hollering, 'Where are you Father? I know you are down there somewhere?' He didn't surface for fifteen minutes . . . he crawled under every table in Bowie . . . he crawled under all the tables. I finally got him up. Here I am with a $95 horse and I am a Protestant and the Catholics didn't bet him."

At Bowie—Charley Eckman, the horse, actually won one in 1973. Charley is far left, the horse is at right, below the jockey.

The Faint of Heart GM

Eckman counts as his friends a host of people from the Back Stretch, many of the top owners, trainers, jockeys and officials from all race tracks on the East Coast. The fact he promotes the sport, knows the game and does a little wagering doesn't hurt his standing with track management.

Eckman: "In the early days of Penn National, while the track was still establishing its reputation, Bill Bork was the general manager. On this night, one of the regulars from Baltimore that I know well comes up to me and asks me to get him a $1,000 loan from the track. He said he didn't have his checkbook with him.

"I know the guy is good for it, so I walked around to the general manager, Bill Bork, and I say this guy wants to make a loan. I vouch that he is a good man, has a solid business and that he will be good for the money. Bork agrees but when I said that he wants a thousand, Bork stopped like I shot him. He said, 'A thou!' He put his hands in his pockets . . . he jumped up and down. He said, 'A thousand! Hold on!' Now, Bork has got his hands in his pockets . . . his thumbs in his belt and he is hollering a thousand! I said, 'Give him the thousand!' Finally, Bork gives the okay.

"Bork tells me, 'Walk behind that son of a bitch . . . walk behind him every moment . . . keep walking behind him . . . don't let him get away.' This fellow hit the triple in the fifth race by picking the first three horses in the correct order of their finish. Bork runs over and says to me, 'He's got twenty-five hundred coming. Get him to sign the papers and get the thousand back!' Now my friend don't want to sign the papers required by the IRS when you win over a certain amount for a single bet.

"After a while, I convinced my friend to sign the document. He goes to the window and gets the money. I walk behind him, get the thousand in cash and I ran it over to Bork. Bork is shaking like a leaf, his face is red from blushing, and he is jumping around. I said, 'Here is that thousand, Bill . . . a thou!' With that, Bork is feelin' rather genial and with a smile on his face, he says to this guy, 'Look, Gene, whenever you need any money, just tell me. We will get it for you. Yeah! We will get it for you.'

"The next day Bork has a heart attack. I just hope that loan didn't bring it on. He pulled out of it and he now is a General Manager at a race track in the Midwest. Bill Bork was a real comedian; he meant well but when it comes to lending money his heart was very, very weak."

The World Series . . . of Handicapping

Several exciting movies have been made about the inherent drama of the greats of billiards and pool, and poker kings in action against one another to determine who is the greatest of the greats. Do you remember "The Cincinnati Kid" and "The Color of Money," and movies of that ilk. With due respect to Steve McQueen, Paul Newman, Tom Cruise and the legendary man with a stick, 'Minnesota Fats,' Eckman has been witness to greater sports drama that didn't even occur in smoke filled rooms.

For twenty years, Eckman had run the greatest, longest-running thoroughbred handicapping contest in America, "The World Series of Handicapping," at Penn National race track outside of Harrisburg, Pennsylvania. A total of $187,500 is at stake in prize money with a cool $100,000 to the winner. To enter the tournament, a contestant is required to ante up $300 for an imaginary $1,000 bank roll. The top 24 contestants in each round with the most imaginary winnings from their imaginary bank roll make it to the finals for the real money and lots of it. No contest money is bet through the mutual windows.

The Penn National "World Series" is the most successful in the country and over the years has increased in value from $5,000 for the winner to the current value. Some one hundred fifty contestants participate each April, May, June, July and August. The finals are held in October with no additional fees to the finalists, but they pay their own expenses. Contestants come from all over America, Canada, Europe, Germany, Israel, and Italy.

In the Harrisburg Sunday, October 28, 1984 issue of the Patriot-News, *writer Roger Quigley described Eckman in action at the World Series of Handicapping.*

"When Charlie Eckman speaks, he speaks. And speaks, and speaks and speaks. 'How ya' been Bernie?' he asks. 'I see you haven't lost any weight.'

"Give him a microphone and his eyes light up. And a smile quickly pastes itself across its face. All except the corner of his mouth which already has been rented to his omnipresent cigar.

"Wherever Eckman goes he commands center stage.

"And this weekend he's holding court on a little stage in the handicappers' area at Penn National Race Course, serving as master of ceremonies for the $160,000 (value in 1984) World Series of Handicapping contest. Eckman keeps the contestants advised of the deadline for making their bets and of other matters of interest. But often it sounds like Don Rickles coming across the speaker.

" 'There they are, the three blind mice standing over there,' is his greeting to three members of the contest's professional contingent."

A Tip From Above

Eckman: "This young lady named Forte and her dad, from outside of Detroit, are in the tournament. In one race, there is a horse called 'Daddy Long Legs' running. The starting odds in the program are thirty-to-one and the odds yo-yo . . . it goes to forty-to-one . . . down to twenty . . . and back up to thirty-to-one.

"This girl bet $992, the balance of her bank roll, on this horse. The imaginary bank roll . . . fun money . . . play money that does not go through the mutual windows. Everybody thought she was foolish, and they were laughing at her. Bingo! The race is on and 'Daddy Long Legs' wins and pays $60 for a $2.00 bet.

"Her winnings put her so far in front that the others in the tournament couldn't find her with a Blood Hound.

"She wins the tournament and on Sunday afternoon I give out the symbolic checks. I'm on the podium with her. A reporter from the ABC program 'Wide World of Sports' is on hand to interview her as the best handicapper.

"The interviewer asked her, 'Why did you bet on a long shot named "Daddy Long Legs?" She said because Jesus Christ told her to do it. Now the place goes silent. You could have heard a pin drop. He said, 'Lady, we are on nationwide TV. I don't think you ought to say something like that.' She said, 'Oh, no. That's the truth. God told me to bet on that horse. I had a tip from God, really! He told me to bet on "Daddy Long Legs!" '

"These race track fanatics were throwing the 'Racing Form' away . . . the 'Morning Telegraph,' track programs . . . everything.

"There is an old Irish guy, who hangs around the track all the time, comes walking behind me. He said, 'Hey, Charley! Did that broad say she had a tip from Jesus Christ?' I said, 'That's what she said.' He said, 'I'll be darned! I'm a good Catholic. I go to confession . . . I go to mass . . . I would have sworn that Jesus Christ had more important things to do than to give out tips at Penn National.'

"Well, that finished us right off. Here we are in the middle of the race track and she is getting the tips from God. Tough to beat, ladies and gentlemen, tough to beat."

The Champ

Some contestants return year after year. The champ of all time is a guy called the "Canadian Kid" Stanley Robinson. Robinson enters five times a year at $300 a contest. In 19 years, he has made the finals just once.

Down to the Wire

Eckman: "One year we had an exceptional final round. On one corner we had the long shots, a young man of Mexican descent from Canada and Chris Thomas, a TV Sportscaster from Baltimore who now works in Tampa, Florida. In the other corner, there are about thirty people ahead of these two in the standings. This includes Andy Byer, a great handicapper for the *Washington Post* newspaper.

"The seventh race is where you have to make your big wager. Now, Thomas is feeling no pain by the time this race comes around. He and the guy from Canada had $600 of their tournament bank roll left each and they didn't care how they bet the money and they take a stab on a long shot. The horse wins and pays $66.

"Just about everyone else had run behind Andy Byer as he went to the window. His horse went from eight-to-one, to two-to-one. They followed him to the window figuring they would get a sure thing tip because Byer is an excellent handicapper. Byer's horse finishes third and this takes care of most of the others in the tournament.

"The Mexican lad from Canada wins the $100,000 top prize and Thomas finishes second and, man, the place was going wild. Here's the kicker. We send the winners their check by mail after the tournament. The guy from Canada just won one hundred grand and I had to loan him $18 to get on the bus to get back home. He didn't have enough real money to go home on.

"Byer was hitting his head against the cement in the race track. The next year, Andy talked the Penn National officials into changing the rules. No longer can a contestant take a long shot with all their contest money. You can only bet a percentage of your bank roll after the seventh race on the last three days of the finals. That means you got to do a little bit of handicapping, not depend on luck."

Eckman attributes the success of the tournament to a great group of people including President Herb Grayek, Phil O'Hara, Vice President and General Manager of Penn National, and Lisa Stokes, Marketing Director.

Starting in 1996, the winner of the "World Series of Handicapping" will receive the Eckman Cup, a stunningly beautiful crystal bowl.

Lisa Stokes (L) and Phil O'Hara (R) hold the Eckman Cup, which will be presented to the World Series of Handicapping winner at Penn National Race Track starting in 1996.

The Pimlico–Laurel Connection

As a devotee of the sport, Eckman is a familiar figure at the Maryland race tracks. He has been friends with some of the great names in Maryland racing, such as the former owners and manager of Pimlico, Ben and Herman Cohen and Chick Lang . . . and the great trainers and jockeys in the circuit of Maryland racing. Many are now a memory just as the tracks are memories too. Gone are the tracks at Bowie and all but one of the half-mile tracks in Maryland . . . Gone are Havre DeGrace, Hagerstown, Marlboro and Bel Air. The only half-mile track to survive is Timonium during the ten days of the Maryland State Fair.

Eckman thought that the Cohens and John Shapiro never received the credit due for their role in Maryland racing. He thought Shapiro's creation of the Laurel International was a great innovation in its time and added to the luster of Maryland racing. Under the Cohen's, the Preakness reached new heights. Eckman said that the man who made it work was Chick Lang. Lang, he said, was "a right guy" and a "class act" who loved racing. But, he added, Chick couldn't do it without the support of the Cohens.

The man responsible for consolidating race track operations in Maryland was the late Frank DeFrancis. Frank, and his son and successor, young Joe, and sister Karen are great personal favorites of Charley's. Charley was also instrumental in getting John Mooney, who was General Manager at Delaware Park, to come down to run the Maryland tracks. According to Eckman, John is an outstanding track administrator.

Charley said, "Mooney knows the ins-and-outs of racing as well or better than any management guy in the business . . . and the young kids, Joe and Karen, are smart and have great heart."

Maryland Racing honored Eckman at the 1991 annual 14th Federico Tesio Banquet for the best in Maryland thoroughbred racing. Charley received a Special Recognition Award.

The program book said of him "Trying to capture Charles Markwood Eckman in print is nearly impossible. Charles is so much a part of Maryland sports, and racing, in particular that a horse 'Motormouth Eckman' was named for him.

"His radio and television commentary is legend. His 'Call a Cab' comment has become synonymous with 'get lost' . . .

" . . . In 1967 he had to give up refereeing basketball when his legs gave out. By then he was already working as a sportscaster at WCBM. He switched to WFBR in 1970. He was named Sportscaster of the Year three times . . .

"Famed as a raconteur, Eckman averaged 50 to 60 speaking engagements a year in the 70's. He has cut down considerably since then.

"A respected handicapper and player of much persistence, Eckman is recognized as being a solid part of the Baltimore scene. He knows everyone. Everyone knows him. He is crabs and beer and is vocal about his affection for thoroughbred racing.

"Eckman retired from different occupations for different reasons. Retirement for Charley only means a change of scenery, not retirement from the limelight."

One of Charley's misfortunes in racing was that "Charley Eckman," a second horse named after him, broke down before becoming the Horse of the Year.

Just before Eckman's legs gave out on the basketball court, he had already launched what would be another very successful career—radio sportscaster.

Chapter

15

Is This What Marconi Had in Mind?

Radio Report: "Earl 'The Pearl' Monroe (NBA Baltimore Bullet star) will shoot from the Mens' Room, if the door is open."

Radio Report: "Paul Blair (the fleet Oriole center fielder) runs after a ball like a rabbit in heat."

Radio Report on the Boston Marathon: "That Jap ran like the bomb was after him." (That observation won a rebuke from the FCC.)

—Charles Markwood Eckman, Jr., Radio Sportscaster

The Start of Something Big

During a meeting, a broadcast executive from another radio station revealed to me, "I spent $25,000 on a survey to find out that Charley Eckman is the number one radio sportscaster in Baltimore. I could have saved the money because I knew that already." And that's the way it was for twenty-three years. Charley and broadcasting were a perfect match.

He was self taught as a referee—a natural. He had no basketball coaching experience but he was a natural. He had no training as a broadcaster. He was a natural. During his broadcasting career, he reached more people than in his other successful careers . . . and he sold more transmission repairs. The only running he had to do was with his mouth . . . which came naturally.

On the air, Charley caused reaction. There was no middle ground. As with Howard Cosell or Rush Limbaugh, audiences loved him or disliked him. Advertisers loved Eckman. A friend of mine, who is in the automobile tire business, once told me, "I've spent a lot of money in radio advertising, but Charley is the only guy who sold tires for me."

Sports columnist Harry S. Russell, *Kent County News*, Chestertown, Maryland wrote about Charley, "Perhaps he doesn't handle the so-called 'King's English' with the polish of a professional orator—he hasn't yet matched Dizzy Dean's 'slud into second base,' though—but he is forthright and knows his sports. If you don't listen, you should."

In his Maryland Diary *Sunday Sun* column under the headline "He's a Charlie Eckman fan," John Goodspeed wrote "In addition to the agonies and the ecstasies that have been inspired this season by the Baltimore Bullets, the Orioles, the Bays and the Colts, a new yes-or-no decision confronts sports fans in this electronic communications area to wit: Do we, or do we not, like Charlie Eckman as a sports commentator?

"Count me in as a Charlie Eckman fan. He turns me on when I turn him on as he analyzes Orioles baseball on television, or fills in with 'color' during the radio broadcasts of Colts football matches—even when he delivers commercials . . .

"In my sporting opinion (as arrogant and righteous as the next fan's), Charlie Eckman is the hottest lecturer to take the field in this circulation area since the advent of Chuck Thompson. Eckman in fact, impresses me as more of an 'original' broadcasting personality, although less of a 'professional' announcer than Chuck Thompson is.

"Thompson, who is probably the best all-around sports announcer now working, is himself more of a broadcasting personality than most sports announcers are.

"And Eckman, to get back to the subject, is more of a professional speaker than many sports fans may imagine. He is a popular after-dinner performer. Success at that trade requires rather more ability with the spoken language that your average sports fan demonstrates when he mouths off in a saloon.

" . . . he avoids the cliches that characterize most sportcasts and, more overwhelmingly, newspaper sports writing. Eckman never resorts to describing a home run as a 'barrier hoist' or a punt return as a 'broken field gallop.'

"He does, on the other hand, allude to fistfights between players and similar emotional disturbances that your standard announcers and sports scribes avoid like the plague. The standard sporting propaganda appeases team owners by implying that the grown men in professional sports never curse or get angry as they earn their living at boys' games. Eckman calls the shots as he sees them, as he might put it.

"Yet he does speak the jargon of players, coaches and know-it-all fans—which differs considerably from the jargon of standard sports writing and broadcasting. Player-coach jargon incorporates straight-English phrases, such as 'a good swing from the right hand side' or 'a smart runner'. But such phrases are inserted in conversation at special places and with special emphasis that reflect years of preoccupation with sports technique. Charlie Eckman apparently speaks this language naturally and fluently. And, unlike many Baltimore-area speakers, who 'choke up' in public, Eckman can ad-lib almost endlessly—in organized paragraphs and complete sentences that are not broken in the middle by pauses.

"Nor is he too technical, a fault of several retired players and coaches who fill in with 'color' during play-by-play broadcasts on the networks. They tend to fill the pauses with 'explanations' that 'we call that play 14 - A - blue.' Eckman 'color' describes what the smart fan is apt to notice, e.g.: 'Again, Johnny U. used Jimmy Orr as your money receiver for that third-down yardage he had to have.' Eckman is more articulate than most coaches and players and more just—folks than most announcers and sports writers. But he is more than a happy medium. In my opinion, a rare and welcome addition to our sporting scene."

There were times Charley reached people in unexpected ways. The following excerpts from a 1965 letter from a non-sports fan from Catonsville, Maryland, illustrates the surprising effect Eckman's broadcasts had on his listeners.

"I have never seen an athletic game during my four years at high school and four years at Cornell. Neither have I ever listened to a sportscaster anywhere without turning to another station. Sports are just of no interest to me—but, the manner in which you present material, has made such a difference that I was contented when my wife, who in her late sixties became an Oriole fan, insisted on hearing each morning as to what had happened to her beloved birds. She recently died suddenly but I got to like your comments although God knows, I know nothing of the business, but it was fun to listen to your terse and what seemed to me, just comments.

Charley has a one day taste of sportcasting in 1947 at WNAV, Annapolis.

"So take this tulip of gratitude from a man to whom baseball is a game where people let balls slip by which they could easily hit if they tried, football a game where 22 stupid men run in the wrong direction, and etc., but I will still listen to your peppery wit."

Another listener during the same year was moved to write praising Charley's defense of the American flag after an athlete showed disrespect. The Reisterstown, Maryland listener wrote, "You hit your mark when you said 'We are becoming tolerant of the intolerable.' Emerson had a good description of some of cowardly me-tooers in evidence today. He calls them the wearers of the gentlest asinine expressions.'"

Columnist Mike Olesker observed in the Baltimore Sun: "There is no record of Eckman's being intimidated—and certainly not inhibited . . .

"His mind is sharp and, of course, quick to formulate opinion. What he has to say is never uttered in a whisper, whether it's behind a studio microphone or before a banquet audience . . . Being around Eckman, even for five minutes, makes you realize that virtually everything he wanted to remember is stored for instant recall."

Eckman became a BMOR (Big Man on Radio) because of the Baltimore Orioles. In 1965, John Kluge's Metromedia purchased WCBM, one of Baltimore's original AM radio stations. John Kelly, the new General Manager, promoted me (Fred Neil) from Assistant News and Sports Director to News and Sports Director.

With 50,000 watts, the authoritative voice of newscaster Galen Fromme, and the Baltimore Orioles broadcasts, rival station WBAL-AM was the top-rated radio station in the Baltimore metropolitan area. Fromme was an institution in Baltimore radio. If he reported that the sky was falling, half the population of Baltimore would have believed him. The other half probably weren't listening.

The Oriole broadcasts dominated the night airwaves. Under the theory that the radio station turned off at night would be the one listened to in the morning, the Metromedia management wanted to break the habit. Kelly wanted to woo that big Oriole broadcast audience to WCBM immediately following the games. He thought that a lively sports talk program after the Oriole games would be the key to the switch. On the other hand, I was interested in someone to replace me as the regular sportscaster at the station.

Kelly asked me who in my opinion had ability to host a high-impact talk program. I had never met Charley. I had only seen him once at a banquet and had watched him referee on several occasions. But, I told Kelly that in Baltimore only Charley Eckman could pull it off. What convinced me was that I had heard Eckman as a frequent guest on a radio talk show.

Once upon a time, WBAL radio had a post game show entitled *"Benny, The Fan, Show."* Benny had a quirky New York personality and a whinny voice. The straight man was Joe Croghan, WBAL's radio sportscaster, who had a terrific voice and lots of style. Eckman stole the show . . . each and every time he appeared. He was loud, brash and funny!

Kelly said to bring him in. Eckman was between engagements and readily agreed to come to the station. Eckman appeared . . . no, no . . . make that he held court . . . before the new WCBM management team. True to character, he was loud, brash and funny. He provided insights into the sports world punctuated with a few vulgarities.

Following the session, Kelly pulled me aside and told me to tape a mock talk show with him as an audition, but to get Charley to repeat some of his stories complete with vulgarities on tape before the mock show. Kelly wanted to send the tape to the Metromedia executives in New York to show them we had a real find . . . and to get them laughing. My request to have Eckman read for the sportscaster job was turned down.

So who listens, right? On the way to the recording studio, I stopped by the newsroom and snatched a United Press International sports brief from the teletype machine.

In the recording studio, I had the engineer run the tape without stopping. I also had one hell of a time getting Eckman to cut loose with his colorful stories with those . . . expletives. After completing the foreplay and the talk show, I asked Charley to read the sports wire copy. Voila! A star is born! He sounded like— Charley Eckman . . . loud, brash and funny . . . and he didn't make mistakes in reading copy.

Having produced and directed radio series with some of the greatest athletes in Maryland sports history . . . Brooks Robinson, John Unitas, Jimmy Orr, Ordell Braase, and Tom Matte . . . Eckman was the only one who could read like a professional broadcaster. The man was ready!

If great stories turn on irony, here is the irony. The talk show never made it to the airwaves . . . but Eckman did, and as my replacement he stayed in broadcasting much longer than I. (I suppose this doesn't have the impact of the Wally Pip–Lou Gehrig story does it?)

When Charley went on the air, it was joked that the station could just throw open its doors because he didn't need a microphone. However, one of Eckman's great strengths was that he is coachable. He was willing to learn and he was a fast learner.

Rim Shot, Please

He learned, for instance, that when you report that a Japanese runner wins the Boston Marathon, you can't say "That Jap ran like the bomb was after him." A listener complained to the Federal Communications Commission (FCC). These were the days before the FCC let their hair down until Howard Stern put it back in curlers. Charley used a lot of insights gained from being in the front line of sports action. He knew basketball . . . "Earl 'The Pearl' Monroe (Baltimore Bullets) will shoot from the Mens' Room, if the door is open." He knew baseball . . . "Paul Blair (the fleet Baltimore Oriole center fielder) runs after a ball like a rabbit in heat." He knew horse racing . . . "Secretariat was so good, the jockey could win riding side saddle." He didn't think Love had any place in public, like on the tennis court.

A New Tip Off

Once in a while, Charley would talk over a story before it aired. For example, the Eli Hanover event. Eli was a popular fight promoter in Baltimore. Late in life, Eli and his wife had a son, their second. Charley was invited to the Jewish religious ceremony for the circumcision that is scheduled seven days after the birth of a boy. It is known as a Bris. In tribute to Eli's prowess—make that "proud accomplishment"—Charley wanted to report on the event . . . delicately. I thought his approach was appropriate for a sport show. Charley reported, "I went to Eli Hanover's son's brisk (sic) at Sinai Hospital today. That's the first time I've seen a clipping without a 15 yard penalty!"

Blind Ambition

A recent graduate from Baltimore City College, Charley's high school alma mater and mine too, applied for a job in my newsroom. He had absolutely no experience. I told the young man, Bobby Johnson, that if he could prove to me that he could be an asset to my newsroom, I would hire him. Hah!

Bobby could monitor our police radios, follow up leads, type like a speed demon, interview and record news personalities, prepare the

Charley's WCBM glamour shot.

news bites with typed lead-ins, tape network feeds, and set them up for broadcast. About the only thing he couldn't do was read wire copy because he was blind. So, I hired him.

Bobby had this extraordinary talent. We would tape the feature race at Laurel and Pimlico and play the tape on the air within five minutes of the finish. Actually, Bobby would handle the taping and walk the tape to the control room. Bobby had this uncanny ability to pick the winner of the race. As the horses were being described during the post parade, Bobby would say, "That horse will win." Nine times out of ten, Bobby's selection would win.

One day, after Bobby picks another winner, Eckman looks at me and says, "We gotta take Bobby to the track!" Several years back, I had won a horse racing contest and a free trip to the Flamingo Stakes for two-year-olds in Miami. The contest was sponsored by Hialeah Race Track in celebration of an anniversary at the track. Eckman has been going to race tracks since the age of six, seven or eight, and, frankly, taught me all I know about handicapping. By golly, now we had discovered the mother lode! We were going to need a Brink's truck to haul all the loot back home. We were taking a young man, who happened to be blind, to Pimlico Race Track to pick winners for us.

In the press box at Pimlico, we read the list of horses entered before each race, and Bobby tells us what he likes. By the fourth race, I had taken a shower and Eckman had taken a bath. Bobby can't pick his nose. Charley is ready to toss Bobby Johnson off the press box balcony. I said, "Bobby, how can you be so good at the station and so bad out here?" Bobby said, "Well, when I record the feature race, I usually remember the winner of the race. When I hear that name again in a race the next week or so, I pick that horse." To which Eckman said, "It's a very simple game!"

Bobby Johnson eventually went to work for the State of Maryland and later owned a number of radio stations.

Colts of Another Color

During the five-year period between 1965 and 1969, I produced the NFL Baltimore Colt play-by-play broadcasts on WCBM. I was also responsible for a series of shows before and after the games and during the season. Some, I just produced, such as "The Buddy Young Show" (one year). One I produced and wrote, "The Tom Matte Show" (two years). Some, programs I produced, wrote and co-hosted "The John

Unitas Pre-Game Show" (four years), "The End Zone with Jimmy Orr" (five years), and "The End Result with Ordell Braase" (five years).

Then, there was the radio version of "Mayhem on 33rd Street," starring Charley Eckman and Art Donovan. For two years, I officiated that production. The show was literally a howling success. It was a funny, irreverent, over-the-top shot from the funny bone look at the over analyzed subject of professional football. With Eckman and Donovan, every subject was fair game and the fair game became very funny stuff.

The show was such a huge success that it was swept away by TV . . . also literally. The TV show lasted several years and died, strangled by the make-up, the need to hit marks, and to watch the camera with the light on, cue cards and the director moving things around. The radio show was free wheeling and unrestricted. As the producer, I would wave at Eckman frantically when a commercial was due. He picked up the cue, read the commercial, and launched back into the verbal mayhem. I would then do what any wise producer should do. I sat back and laughed.

Eckman would try anything . . . once.

Theoretically, the show should not have worked at all. Both Charley and Art Donovan are very funny men, but with very different styles. Both were better suited to work with straight men who could set them up. But, Eckman was too smart to waste Donovan's talent. He liked Artie and respected him.

I also think that Donovan genuinely appreciated Charley, the ex-referee. Donovan's father was one of the most respected men in professional boxing, a world class referee. What Donovan appears to be when he appears on the David Letterman TV show is exactly what Donovan is. Anything good you may have heard about Artie—double it! He is the genuine article.

In his younger days, Donovan had a prodigious appetite. A new sponsor, a pizza restaurant, sent two 16-inch pizzas to the station for us to sample. Charley, the engineer and I shared one. Artie sampled the entire other one.

Artie was a walking advertisement for Hebrew National products. He loved the big, kosher hot dogs. Once, we were at a Father and Son Night event where they served Artie's favorite hot dogs. Artie was driving up to New York that night and he asked me to check with one of the hosts and see if the guy could get Artie a dozen hot dogs to eat on the way. Before the host I asked came back from the kitchen, another one of the hosts brought Artie a bag and said "Mr. Donovan, here are the dozen hot dogs you wanted for the trip." If Eckman was right, the two dozen hot dogs were Artie's pay for appearing.

The Eckman—Donovan TV Connection

Eckman and Donovan on TV produced a lot of laughs, and not all of them on the show.

> Eckman: "Artie and I are doing a commercial for a car dealer. Well, I'm rattlin' off the copy and Donovan is suppose to hit me with the pie at the end of the commercial and say 'tell them Artie sent you.' Well, I start the thing off and get to my cue line which was 'tell them Charley sent you!'
>
> "I'm waitin' for Artie to hit me with a pie and say his line. Now, the cameras are all grinding away and Artie is just standing there. I said, 'What the hell are you doing Donovan? Throw that pie or we will be here all day.
>
> "He says, 'Cholly, I was just listenin' to you.' I said 'You ain't

suppose to listen to me, dummy! You are suppose to throw that pie at me.' Well, we start off again with the cameras rolling. I say the cue line again, 'tell them Charley sent you!' Donovan let's me have it. He hit me so hard that the pie, crust and all, went all across the room and hit the back of the studio. I saw stars and I looked like a fugitive from a Mack Sennett comedy.

"Then Donovan hollers, 'Oh! I got you! I got you! You big mouth son of a bitch!' All he was suppose to say was 'tell 'em Artie sent you.'"

Turkey Hawks

Eckman: "One of the gimmicks on the TV show was an on-air bet. We had a 'Game of the Week' thing in which I would pick one team to win and Artie would pick the other.

"The loser would have to perform some crazy stunt. One week, Donovan loses and we have to go do something at a turkey farm in Howard County. While we are out there Donovan decides to pick a turkey up for Thanksgiving for the Valley Country Club, a place he and his wife own.

"There we were walking through this turkey farm. We ain't never seen a turkey farm or a turkey that wasn't frozen, I don't think. Well, now they are all around us. There is one big bird Donovan is really looking at. The turkey is looking at Donovan too. The next thing you know the bird pecks Donovan on the top of his head.

"Donovan says, 'Cholly, that turkey just bit me!' I said, 'Well, nail him, Donovan. We're bigger than him. Show him who's boss. Knock him on his ass.' Artie says, 'I'm going to bust his ass!' With that, he turns around and popped that turkey and that turkey went down with a thud.

"And then . . . all of his buddies came a runnin'. Fifteen-hundred turkeys came at us. Donovan hollers, 'I think we'd better get outta' here!' Now, we are running through that barn-yard and we are running as fast as we can run. Those turkeys are runnin' after us as fast as they could run and squawkin' like wild birds. What a racket! We get to the end of this lane and get that fence closed. We were sweating like horses.

"The old farmer, who owned the place, says to us, 'What the hell did you guys do stirring up my birds like that?! They will loose all their fat!' I said, 'Yeah! . . . and Donovan would loose his damn head if we'd have stayed out here much longer.' It was a very precarious afternoon."

As News and Sports Director at WCBM, I hired Richard Sher, a young Baltimorean who was working at a small Washington, D.C. metropolitan radio station, as a member of my news staff. Richard and Charley got to know each other during this period. Sher eventually joined the Baltimore Westinghouse station, WJZ-TV, news staff and he has hosted a number of talk shows. He co-hosted a program for many years with Oprah Winfrey. Sher frequently featured Charley on his "Sound Off" show and others. At times, Artie Donovan was a guest on the same show. Each time Charley and Artie appeared on the air together, they played off each other and the laughs flew!

The Return of Joe Croghan

For the 1969 pro football season, Eckman was paired with Joe Croghan for the Baltimore Colt broadcasts. By then Joe, who had been the top radio sportscaster in Baltimore, had been working for a Miami station for a number of years. Joe is articulate, urbane and dresses as if he stepped out of the pages of *Gentlemen's Quarterly*. He always wore a tie.

Only once during that year do I remember Joe being less than impeccably dressed. Enroute from California Polytechnic College, where the Colts were holding forth between games with the San Diego Chargers, the Oakland Raiders, and the Houston Oilers, Joe and I stopped at the exclusive restaurant at the famed Pebble Beach Golf Course. Joe snickered because he didn't think I could get in without a tie. He was wearing his tie, but, I snickered last because they wouldn't let him in either because he wasn't wearing a jacket.

Joe would fly in from Miami, arriving the day prior to the game. Charley would usually fly in with the Colts from Baltimore. I would always arrive on a weekday to review the set up for the broadcasts, particularly for the locker room show with Jimmy Orr that was broadcast immediately after the game.

Shufflin' Off To Buffalo

Joe wore a microphone harness around his neck. This enabled him to turn to face the action for the play-by-play without concern for the position of the mike. The Colts played the Buffalo Bills in the old War Memorial stadium in Buffalo, where the motion picture "The Natural" was filmed. Our assigned broadcast booth in this old stadium was very compact. Poor lighting left both end zones in semi-darkness. Joe would lean over to see the action and in the process would bounce into Charley on the right. I was sitting on Eckman's left with the commercials, promotions, and the station breaks. I would bounce into him every time I reached over to give him or Joe the copy. At times, I would poke Charley to get his attention.

By half time, Joe and I had hit Charley more times than Moe hit Curley in all the Three Stooges movies. During a commercial break, Eckman said, "The next time one of you guys hits me, I'm going to make like Joe Louis and one of you will be the next Max Schmelling."

Adventures in the Big Easy

Then there was the exhibition game held in New Orleans that year. The night before, we had enjoyed the hospitality of that great city with a big assist from a Canadian Club. Charley stayed up later than we did, and didn't make it to the team bus. He arrived at Tulane stadium by cab just before game without benefit of breakfast. Charley wouldn't have a chance to eat until after his halftime interview.

Our very narrow broadcast booth was in the end zone curve at the top of the stadium. The booth was not connected with the regular press box and the wind currents cause the door to slam if not closed by hand. Joe was dressed meticulously, as usual. Charley was starving and couldn't wait until we had cleared halftime.

Charley came back from the press box after the second half started with a mile high sandwich and a tall brew in a paper cup. To get through the door, he placed the cup on the paper plate with the sandwich. The plate was one of the tri-divided type that had curved compartments. Charley came through the door holding the plate as a tray. As he closed the door slowly, the change in the wind direction caused the wind to hit the cup and it jumped off the plate and flipped over the nattily attired Joe Croghan. After a short but pithy beat, Joe picked up on the play-by-play through his clenched teeth. Croghan slowly turned to face Eckman. Joe's short Irish fuse had been lit. The beer began to steam from his ever redding neck. The look in Joe's eyes could have started a forest fire.

Charley looked down at me from my position of hysterical laughter on the floor, and mouthed the words, "Did you push me?" Then, a very contrite Charles M. Eckman pulled out his handkerchief and proceeded to very, very carefully mop Croghan's face, neck, hair, glasses, collar, tie, and coat. He even offered Joe his sandwich all the while mouthing his apologies.

WCBM ad. Charley (L), Eckman (R).

By the end of the third quarter, Joe was partially dry, the chill was leaving his voice, he no longer was calling the game through his teeth, and the red was subsiding in his neck. As if a light turned on, Joe suddenly realized how ridiculous this looked. He started breaking up on the air and he had to fight to keep his composure for the remainder of the game. Charley's "color" on the remainder of the broadcast was the lack of it in his face, his remorse and explanation of what had happened. Occasionally, he turned to me while I was still trying to muffle my laughter, and asked if I was sure that I hadn't pushed him.

In the parking lot after the game, Joe and Charley buried the Club, Canadian variety, or what was left of the bottle and laughed like hell. Amazingly, Joe showed up for the reminder of the season. Eventually, he moved back to Baltimore, but that's another story.

Shrimpy Toast

If there is a Hall of Fame for the most mouth watering commercial in radio, Eckman's commercial for Joe Louie's New Sea Girt Inn would be safely ensconced. When he described the restaurant's version of Shrimp Toast that he called Shrimpy Toast, he gave new meaning to the Pavlovian theory.

Enter a new Sales Manager at WCBM, Bill Lauer. Bill was a super guy, very fair, and a by-the-book businessman. He noticed that the restaurant had been on the air for two years but had never signed a contract and Bill wanted a contract in hand.

Eckman would ad-lib most of the commercials for the restaurant, a regular haunt for Charley and his family. In fact, Charley had never solicited the owner to advertise. It was the "proud proprietor," Joe Louie, who had approached Eckman.

> Eckman: "One day, while paying the bill, Joe says he wants to go on the air with me. I said, 'Fine, Joe. What do you want me to say?' He said, 'You talk!' I said, 'OK!' I ad-libbed the commercial . . . the whole minute. 'Joe Louie's New Sea Girt Restaurant . . . that Shrimpy Toast will melt in your mouth . . . get that Shrimpy Toast.'"

During the first two years the restaurant is on the air with Eckman, the Shrimp Toast became very popular and helped make Joe Louie a millionaire in due time. The owner did his part by paying his bills promptly.

Now, Lauer insists that Mr. Louie had to have a contract. Charley invites Lauer to have dinner there to resolve the issue. During dinner, Lauer introduces himself and says with a stern look, "I understand you don't have a contract with Charley or WCBM." Joe Louie looks at him and says, "Me no need no contract."

> Eckman: "Lauer says, 'You have to have a contract to be on the air.' I said, 'Bill, what are you going to do . . . throw him off the air because he pays his bills? . . . what the hell is this all about? 'Bill says to Joe, 'I can't understand this. You don't have a contract. You don't know what Charley is saying on the air, and you are happy?' Joe says, 'That's right. Charley talk 'em. Joe pay 'em . . . that's all.' With that, Joe walks away from us.
>
> "I said, 'Now, are you going to throw him off the air?' 'No,' Lauer said, 'I'll never believe it. I won't believe it. Yet, I'm going to believe it. I'm going to sit here and I'm going to go with Joe Louie and Charley Eckman. Joe said, 'No contract . . . Charley talk 'em . . . Joe pay 'em . . . the hell with the rules, let's go!.'"
>
> "So, that's how we kept Joe Louie on the air. We never had a contract. He was on the air with me for eighteen years on WCBM and WFBR."

WCBM underwent a radical change in direction. Kelly was gone. A new Program Director tossed out Steve and Edie, Barbra, Nat, Frank, and even the King Sisters, ouch! Suddenly, the station wasn't fun any more. Charley was ready to march on.

Chapter

16

Enlisted in the First Broadcasting Regiment

" 'I wanted some personalities on this station and Charlie was the biggest personality in the town,' says Harry Shriver, general manager of WFBR radio, who hired Eckman in 1970. 'Everybody knew Charlie Eckman . . . .'

"In 1970, Eckman jumped to WFBR for a $50-a-week raise. His gravelly voice and his barbs at the sporting community—and his malapropisms—were legendary," wrote Annapolis *reporter Paul Girsdansky,* The Sunday Capital *some 17 years later.*

" 'He was a free spirit,' says Harry Shriver. "There have been moments when I wanted to strangle him. He's in a business that's heavily regulated and very controllable.

"Even if Eckman sounded like a loose cannon on the air, he was in command of himself and his, ahem, colorful language.

" 'When Charlie goes into a studio and sits in front of a microphone, he presses a button and turns off all that language. He knows when to be uninhibited and when not to be," Shriver says . . ."

Charley came to me and said he heard that WFBR was interested in his services. In all due respect to WBAL and their 50,000 watts, the hottest news rivalry in town was between WCBM and WFBR, whose call letters stood for the First Broadcasting Regiment. Along with WBAL and WCBM, WFBR was one of the four original radio stations in Baltimore. Unfortunately, time and FM radio have not been kind to AM radio. Baltimore lost a part of its heritage when the WFBR call letters were dropped.

I called a respected colleague at WFBR, Tom Marr, who denied the interest, but who listened attentively. I indicated that Charley was receptive and told him what it would take to get Charley to his station. Charley stayed there for eighteen years as the sports director of the station. WFBR won the rights to the Oriole Broadcasts and created a brilliant promotional campaign for the team and the broadcasts. Occasionally, Charley was an added color commentator on the broadcasts.

Eckman: "I'm working the game with Chuck Thompson, who is now in the Baseball Hall of Fame in Cooperstown, and the late Bill O'Donnell. They were doing the play-by-play. With some notable exceptions, like Harry Caray with the Cubs, play-by-play announcers try to be neutral in giving their description.

"This night, I'm in the booth and the Orioles are locked in a terrific game. I got caught up in the excitement when third baseman Doug DeCinces hit a long ball that would win it for us if the ball goes out. I get up in the booth and I'm hollering, 'Get out of here! Get out of here! Get out of here!' And the ball goes out of the park and we win. I remember where I am and I look around.

Charley (L) during 1982 WFBR broadcast with Frank Deford.
(Photo by Janis Rettaliata.)

Chuck Thompson loved it, but Bill O'Donnell would have preferred that I would do what the Swiss do. Stay quietly neutral."

His WFBR boss Shriver reported that the taped replay of Eckman's "call" of the DeCinces home run was requested more than any music record the station had on the air for several weeks.

On radio, Eckman had them laughing, but like his officiating career, he wasn't everybody's glass of chilled Chardonnay. On the air, Eckman will admit that his style of sportscasting divided the listening public into opposite camps—those who loved him, and those who didn't. But one thing was certain, Charley could sell.

Even the staid Business Section of *Baltimore Sun* covered Eckman in an article on March 14, 1974 with the headline, *"With love, or hate, Charlie does a great selling job."*

"Thomas E. O'Neill, president of Vermont Federal Savings & Loan Association thinks the world of Charlie Eckman.

" 'Little children send their fathers in here with $4 and $5 to open accounts just because they heard Charlie on the air . . . People either hate him or love him, but they listen to him,' Mr. O'Neill adds. 'He's a great salesman,' vows Bruce S. Dunham, of Doner Advertising. 'I was with him one night when he was guest at the American Legion Hall in Dundalk. When he walked in, it was like the second coming of Christ.'

"So potent a salesman is Charlie Eckman that sponsors are waiting in line for space on his four-time daily radio show . . .

"All in all, estimates Harry Shriver, manager of WFBR, Mr. Eckman brings in $100,000 a year.

"The guy on the street

"Charlie Eckman—salesman, sportscaster, horse player—is not for everybody, as Charlie Eckman is the first to attest. His sales technique is most effective in Sparrows Point, Dundalk and Glen Burnie. 'I talk the average guy's language, 'Mr. Eckman says, 'I'm more or less the guy on the street.' ' . . . when you're advertising with the guy. He's probably the hottest advertising property in the state.' "

Charley's Kids

Charley's early years instilled in him an inner drive to help young people. This letter received by WFBR is typical of Charley's efforts. In public, Eckman held court. However, he also gave back to the community without fanfare. Typical was this reaction from Robert J. Rattell, who had arranged for a series of guest lectures at Mt. St. Joseph's High School. He wrote to WFBR General Manager Harry Shriver in June 1993.

"Charley spoke on the topic 'The Importance of Enthusiasm,' . . . and he did an excellent job in presenting his views and in reinforcing what the students were being taught.

"He accepted the invitation, asking no monetary compensation despite his busy and rigorous professional schedule.

"We feel that such unselfishness and dedication to our youth should not go unnoticed . . ."

Charley was frequently involved in projects that helped people in need of caring. His efforts in working with the Benedictine School and the Tri-County Special Olympics on the Eastern Shore of Maryland were generally unheralded along with many similar endeavors. For many years he served as the Honorary Chairman of the Baltimore Association of Retarded Citizens Bar-B-Que, at the time the principal fund raiser for that organization.

Charley didn't forget Senior Citizens in need of a few laughs either. Father Neil O'Donnell sent the following letter to Shriver at WFBR.

"Last Tuesday I had the pleasure of being with Charley Eckman at a Halloween costume party at Jenkins Memorial—a Catholic sponsored residential facility for the aged and chronically ill.

"I would like to compliment Mr. Eckman, first of all for his acceptance of the invitation and secondly for his concerned interest and attention to the residents. The institutionalized aged and chronic ill are a neglected group in our society. On several occasions in the past, the administration of Jenkins Memorial have invited people from the community to various affairs. The invitations were mostly rejected and frequency ignored. Charley Eckman's attendance and participation, in his own inimitable way, turned a small in-house party into a gala occasion. His visit will be long remembered and Charley and WFBR gained many friends.

"In my capacity as Director of the Division of Health Affairs, Archdiocese of Baltimore, I extend my gratitude for this consideration."

Broadcasting a Blast

One of Eckman's favorite sports was soccer. He had the opportunity to kick it around on the air. He handled the color on the WFBR broadcasts of the Baltimore Blast of the Major Indoor Soccer League. He teamed with Art Sinclair who did the play-by-play. Charley, as usual, had a blast . . . but the fans listening to his commentary may have had a larger one.

In typical Eckman fashion, he learned to pronounce the various slavic names. But, unlike his broadcasting stints with the Colts and the Orioles, Charley did enter the locker room and he got to know and developed a rapport with the players and the coach. He didn't hold back criticism when it was warranted and he created excitement on the air.

Charley's love for soccer was evident in his colorcast duties. Charley and Blast Coach Kenny Cooper became close friends.

Cooper was amazed by Eckman's remarkable ability to meet someone he personally knew in every city they visited. Eckman bet that during their travels with the team, he would always—always know someone.

For 74 away trips in a row with the Blast, Charley met in arenas, restaurants, hotels, airports or on the street one or more acquaintances. For Kenny, to meet someone you know during 74 trips in our huge country was unfathomable.

The record was about to end in Phoenix, Arizona. Charley's broadcast partner, Art Sinclair, proclaimed the streak was officially over as the team boarded the airplane. Charley was pacing back and forth by the boarding counter trying to find someone he knew. Nothing, nobody,

Charley (L) shakes hands with Blast Coach Kenny Cooper (R), surrounded by Blast players. (Photo by Janis Rettaliata.)

Cooper remembers. Charley, he said, looked crest fallen. As the trio were the last to board the plane, a voice shouted, "Charley, is that you?" Eckman roared back at the pilot, "Dale Smith. Who in the —— do you think it is?"

On another occasion in Phoenix, Cooper and Blast official Drew Forester spotted a glum Eckman in the lobby of the team hotel late one evening. Eckman, glum? They knew something had to be wrong. Concerned, they prodded Charley into telling them the reason.

Charley always played his celebrity status to the hilt. He decided to dine in the hotel alone that evening and another diner saluted him with his champaign glass. Charley thought the guy must know who he was and invited him over to his table for dinner. Throughout the evening, Charley regaled his visitor and anyone else in the restaurant within earshot with his basketball stories. Charley made a strong contribution

A Charley Eckman kick-off starts a Blast indoor soccer game. (Photo by Janis Rettaliata.)

to the whiskey industry of Scotland while his new found friend liberated a lot of champaign bubbles.

The guy suggested that they cap the evening off with a drink at the bar. Eckman thought the man was going to pick up the tab for the huge dinner they had just eaten and he agreed. After ordering another round of drinks at the bar, the "friend" excuse himself to visit the Men's Room. When the bill was delivered to Charley, he told the waitress to wait until his friend returned.

After a while, he sent a Bus Boy into the Men's Room to check on the guy. The room was empty. The Desk Clerk said that the man had left the hotel and Charley got stuck with a bill for $214. This was probably the only time Eckman had ever been taken and it was a day that Cooper will never forget.

Eventually, the "Blast" folded but Eckman returned to do color on TV with the new team, "The Spirit," in the new indoor soccer league. Sandra McKee, *Baltimore Sun* sports writer reported:

"Like Wittman, Eckman gives Spirit familiar look, HTS team includes Davis, Mangione, It was a day for blasts from the past."

"On the same day the Baltimore Spirit announced it was signing former Blast star Tim Wittman, the National Professional Soccer League team introduced Charlie Eckman as the commentator on its eight game Home Team Sports package yesterday . . .

" 'I tell you, I'm happy to be back,' said Eckman . . . 'I missed it. I love the action. When I was growing up here in the '30s and '40s, baseball was the number one sport and soccer was number two,' Eckman said.

" 'Soccer still has some skill in it, and this new league has potential with its scoring system.'

"Eckman said, 'It's going to get people talking. When they hear about an 18-15 soccer score, they're going to want to come see the game . . .' "

Even off the air Charley was into soccer. Charley's love of soccer and kids were blended in the summer of 1982 when the American Legion Post 38 Under 19 Soccer Team represented the United States and won an international tournament. Paul M. Scardina, the Head Coach of the team wrote to WFBR. ". . . The parents organized a homecoming party for our return on July 16. Among the guests was Mr. Eckman. On this occasion he spoke very highly of our team and the boys and promised that he would see to it that we received the recognition that he thought we deserve.

"True to his word, On July 27, he sponsored a banquet that I and members of my team and accompanying friends will never forget. He arranged the donation of individual trophies to each of my boys, along with trophies for my entire coaching staff, the coordinating committee responsible for raising the funds for our trip, and the American Legion Club itself. He also served as our Master of Ceremonies. It was a great honor for us and a night we will never forget, and Mr. Eckman is the person responsible for it all . . ."

For 23 years Eckman regularly titillated, scandalized, amused, and amazed his listeners. And there were frequent personal, banquet and television appearances.

FBI's Most Wanted

On one of Charley's TV appearances he took on the Baltimore office of the FBI and in the process, stunned Al Sanders, the new evening news anchor of WJZ, the Westinghouse Television station in Baltimore. The station, Channel 13, featured guest commentators on the early news segment.

The FBI had started an investigation into American League Baseball Umpires whose names were found in the little black book of an alleged bookmaker, Al Isella. Isella also happened to be the Maitre' D of a very popular (and very good) restaurant in Baltimore's Little Italy, Sabatino's.

Professional athletes know the finest restaurants in any town, and "Sabby's" was definitely an "in" spot. Eckman went on the air to proclaim that the FBI was nuts to think that these umpires were involved in any hanky panky. Charley reasoned that Isella had the names in his book because, like other human beings, the umpires liked good food, and Isella listed them for red carpet treatment for tables and service. He closed his argument by stating, "These umpires wouldn't gamble. I know them all . . . and they're too cheap to bet!" Reportedly, Sanders eyes got bigger and bigger as Charley delivered his commentary.

Sanders, who passed away as a result of cancer in 1995, became a phenomenally popular news anchorman. Shortly before he left the air, he was the guest speaker at one of the monthly graduations at the internationally renowned Maryland Rehabilitation Center. The Center, one of only 11 comprehensive state rehabilitation centers for individuals with disabilities, is operated by the Division of Rehabilitation Services, Maryland State Department of Education. The Division provides a variety of services designed to assist its adult clients enter or return to competitive employment.

Sanders could not have been more gracious on that day. He stayed after the ceremonies to sign autographs and give hugs to students who requested one and/or the other. He confirmed what Charley had previous told me. Charley not only caused Al to raise his eyebrows on his first telecast at WJZ, but Eckman took him around town and introduced him to a lot of people, VIPs and blue collar residents. Sanders said that with Eckman he learned a lot about the heart of the city and being with Charley certainly didn't hurt the ratings.

In 1987, Eckman formally retired from WFBR. John Steadman, the highly respected, award-winning Sports Editor of the *News American*, who became a columnist for *The Evening Sun*, gave him a send off. In his Friday, June 26, 1987 column, with the headline, "Eckman calls a cab, and rides off into the sunset," John Steadman wrote, "Nothing was ever gift-wrapped for Charley Eckman, who found that the steep bridge to success was locating a radio station that would power his words to a listening public that either had to become conditioned to the shock treatment he purveyed or else turn him off. Being soft-spoken or tentative wasn't his style.

Eckman (L) was a frequent guest on WJZ, Channel 13. Here, with Sports Anchor John Kennely.

"The Eckman you heard on radio is the same one you meet at the race track, on the street corner or in a restaurant—brash, bold and brackish."

Sun columnist Mike Olesker on June 30, 1987 put it this way: "Charley Eckman shuts off his mike and calls a cab . . . For Eckman, who shuts down his WFBR radio microphone after two decades, life has always been a very simple game . . . 'I became a referee because I was hungry.' he said once. 'It beat stealing.'

"So does radio announcing. He's 65 now and said yesterday he's quitting the business because, 'I'm tired of getting up at a quarter to five.'"

Of course, Eckman, who retired more times than George Burns, and from more occupations, never really did retire. Charley returned to host a talk program on WCBM after that station had undergone several changes of ownership. Unfortunately, it cut into his social security checks and he re-retired . . . sort of.

Charley still managed to do many commercials and frequently appeared as a guest on radio and television shows. He was a popular frequent guest during the baseball season on the "Baseball and Boog" TV Show, starring former Oriole great Boog Powell, and "Donovan, Braase and Friends," featuring former Baltimore Colts Artie Donovan and Ordell Braase. Once again, Artie and Charley clicked on the air. The host of both shows is Tom Davis, who became a great friend of Charley's.

Eckman's life has many facets, like a diamond . . . like a baseball diamond. A flash back is in order.

Chapter

17

Bugle Call

"The Washington Elite Giants had a hard-hitting first base-man by the name of 'Mule' Suttles. Joe Cambria had the ball park fences placed far out so he wouldn't lose many balls over the fences. 'Mule' hit the longest ball ever hit at Bugle Field. It cleared the center field fence 456 feet away on the rise. The ball he hit was the worst constructed ball used in the professional baseball. The brand name of the ball he hit was 'Worth.' It should have been named 'Worthless.'"

"Suttles was huge. He weighed well over 300 pounds. The only way to find out how much he really weighed was to put him on a meat scale. 'Mule' wore a bedroom slipper on his left foot and baseball spikes on his right. A sportswriter asked him why? 'Mule' answered, 'My feet hurt.' It's a very simple game!"
—Charles Markwood Eckman, Jr., Bat Boy

Eckman's career on the baseball diamond actually started at the age of twelve. Before Charley's father died in 1933, he would take Charley to Oriole Park at 29th Street and Greenmount Avenue and to Bugle Field to see professional baseball. Bugle Field was located at the end of the world—what seemed like the end of the world to Charley—at the end of Federal Street at Loney's Lane, now known as Sinclair Lane, in Northeast Baltimore. Charley and Charley, Senior, would take the streetcar nicknamed the "Toonerville Trolley" after the vintage comic strip. The route ended at Bugle Field, now the home of the Lord Baltimore Press.

Eckman's love of the game was kindled in those days with his Dad. Bugle Field became a source of income as well as a source of entertainment.

A remarkable man by the name of Joe Cambria became an important part of young Charley's life. Cambria owned the Bugle Coat and Apron Company in Baltimore. Joe was a scout for the Washington Senators and the owner of three minor league teams in professional baseball, each with the moniker of the Senators. The highest ranking team was the International League Triple A Albany Senators (New York State), followed by the Harrisburg Senators (Pennsylvania) and the Salisbury Senators (Maryland) in the Eastern Shore Class D League. He also owned one of the best—if not the best—baseball teams in the old Negro league, the Baltimore Black Sox, that used Bugle Field as the home field.

At first, young Charley used his street smarts before he became a "regular" for Cambria.

> Eckman: "I would go down to Bugle Field at night with a couple of newspapers, the old green edition of the *Baltimore Post*. I would buy them for four cents and sell them to people at the ballpark for a nickel or a dime, and watch the game for nothing. I thought I died and had gone to heaven."

But, baseball heaven was still to come. Cambria took a liking to Charley, hired him to help on a company delivery truck and made him a bat boy for two of his teams: The Black Sox and the Albany Senators when that team came to play the Orioles, in the International League. The Black Sox duties were split with others, but when he wasn't bat boying, he was a ball chaser. In that capacity, he would chase down balls hit out of the ball park and return them to the team. He got a quarter a game.

The Black Sox Bat Boy

How in the world, you might ask, did a little white kid get to be bat boy for a black baseball team?

> Eckman: "I got to be bat boy for a two reasons. First, the Black Sox played at Bugle Field in a white neighborhood. Second, I needed the money. My dad was not working because of him

being gassed during World War I. He was in and out of the hospital a lot. Joe Cambria used to talk to me at the ballpark and we became very friendly. I got that quarter a game from Dick Lundy, who was the manager and short stop for the team."

Eckman saw the game from the ground up and ended as a baseball scout for 16 years. In addition to the greats of the era on the Negro League and the International League, he saw many of the best National and American Major League players who barnstormed on All-Star teams. In those days, major leaguers found barnstorming a way to keep the roof over their heads and groceries on the table during the winter months.

Charley maintains that Bugle Field was the best baseball diamond in Baltimore thanks to Matt Reinholt, the groundskeeper. The field was in better shape than the Orioles' park on 29th Street and Greenmount Avenue. As a result, baseball games were played at Bugle Field until late Fall.

Eckman: "As the bat boy, I hung around the ball park all day in the summer during the Black Sox's practice. They would play three or four games a week against teams like the Birmingham Giants, Pittsburgh Crawfords, the Kansas City Monarchs, the Washington Elite Giants, the Homestead Grays, the Philadelphia Stars, and the New York Black Yankees."

"The Washington Elite Giants had a pitcher named McDonald who was a submarine pitcher. He would come over the side so far that he would scrape his knuckles against the ground. The Elite Giants team later moved to Baltimore.

"The best black team that ever played in the the state of Maryland, maybe one of the best teams I have ever seen, were the Baltimore Black Sox teams around 1930 through 1932. Dick Seay, a Cuban, played second base. At first base was "Showboat" Thomas who came down from the New York Black Yankees. The third baseman was a guy named Findley. The Black Sox had two of the finest catchers I ever saw as a kid or an adult. 'Eggy' Clark could throw the ball sitting on his haunches from behind the plate. I mean, he had a cannon for an arm. 'Big' Casey was a left-handed hitting catcher that the Baltimore Black Sox got from the Philadelphia Stars. Any major league team today would love to have either one of these guys. Believe me, a lot of black ballplayers on the Black Sox could

At age 18, All-Maryland with Mt. Washington team, 1938-39.

have been in the big leagues at that time.

"The Black Sox had three real good outfielders who could go get the ball and hit with power. In right field was Buddy Burbage, who ran like a deer. He was a pretty good ball player. In center field was a guy named Washington and the left fielder was 'Crush' Holloway. The Williams boys come up and played the year after I became the bat boy. They were terrific players.

"The team had a fellow named 'Slim' Jones who could pitch. He could throw aspirins. Norman Yokely, a Baltimore guy, was an outstanding pitcher, but he hurt his arm and did not pitch much after the injury. Before he got hurt, Yokely would pitch in the All-Star games against the white major leaguers after the regular season. Yokely had a major league arm. Yokely could have been a great big league pitcher because he had hands bigger than hams. His hands were so big, that a batter could not see the ball until he started throwing it."

The Cuban Imposter

Professional baseball was segregated at that time. Cubans could play in major leagues but blacks could not. So Joe Cambria tried to help Norman Yokely make it to the majors by passing him off as a Cuban. Cambria would send Norman down to Norfolk, or Newport News, Virginia, put him on a freighter, pay for the passage and try to get him into the port of Baltimore as a Cuban. This must have happened five or six times, but Norman never made it through as a Cuban. He never got a chance to play in the Majors, but he played against white Major League players.

The Black Sox Versus the Major League All-Stars

Many of the top major and minor league white ball players came through Baltimore to play a series of games against the Black Sox.

Eckman: "The Black Sox would play against guys like Joe Kuhel, from the Washington Senators, after his team won the pennant in 1933. Others who came were George Puccinelli, and Yankees like Don Heffner and Jake Powell, the great Hack Wilson from the Cubs. Wilson was near the end of his career when he came. Jack Russell, the pitcher, and the Weaver boys, Jim and Monte, would all come down and play at Bugle Field. Lester Bell from up in Harrisburg, a real good infielder who played with the St. Louis Cardinals, would play. Buzz Arlett, an outstanding minor league hitter, would come.

"The Black Sox would round out their team by bringing in really good players from the Pittsburgh Crawfords. The Homestead Grays would lend some of their best players including 'Always Mad' Wilson, a first baseman. He was called 'Always Mad' because he was always mad with everybody . . . blacks, whites, and grays."

Jokin' Jack Powell

It was "better than the movies" when Jake "Rabbit" Powell came to town. Jake was a frequent barnstormer on All Star teams that played against the Black Sox at Bugle Field. And Jake became a favorite of Charley. Powell was from the Washington, D.C. area.

When he was on the Albany Senators team, he played against the Orioles in the International League.

Eckman: "Jake Powell was the lead-off hitter for the Albany Senators. He gets locked up in Baltimore by the police prior to a game. Well, Jake gets released from jail and comes flyin' in moments before the game starts. He puts on Ray Prim's uniform, a left-handed pitcher, who later played with the Washington Senators. He walks up to the plate with no batting practice . . . no warm up.. no nothin'! The Orioles are already on the field.

"Here comes the first pitch . . . Bop! . . . out of the ballpark! . . . a home run. He circles the bases and he's yellin' at his bench, 'I told you guys I don't need to practice with you' . . . and then he runs back into the clubhouse. The next year he goes to the New York Yankees.

"One year the Yankees win the pennant, Jake comes home to Washington and blows his whole World Series check, eight grand, in an illegal gambling club named Jimmy Fontaine's—in one night.

"Once when Powell was playing on this All-Star team against the Black Sox at Bugle Field, he decides to have a little mischief at the expense of the Umpire, Wharton Drury, who was working behind home plate.

"At that time, the Umpire behind the plate would wear this big inflatable chest protector on the outside of their uniform. The outside chest protector is much better than the protector worn inside the coat because the Umpire can look over the catcher's shoulder, or over his head. That way, the Umpire can call both sides of the plate. Today, they work inside or outside of the plate with the inside chest protector and they don't see enough of the plate to give accurate calls of balls and strikes. I'll tell you, Umps today don't have as much guts as them old timers did . . . because the old timers had a big bag in front of them and they didn't get hurt. They were better on balls and strikes then the present day umpires . . . and I am not exaggerating.

"Powell is scheduled to lead off. Secretly, he had unscrewed the air valve so that the air would slowly come out of Drury's chest protector. Now, Drury is at the plate during the exchange of the line-up cards and explaining the ground rules. The air is slowly leaking out of the bag and Drury doesn't notice it as he picks up his chest protector puts it on and hollers, 'Play Ball!'

"I'm the bat boy, and Powell says to me, 'Watch, this kid,' and he heads up to the plate to lead off the game. Now, Jake whispers to the catcher to let the first pitch go. The pitcher is 'Slim Jones' who really throws bullets. The first pitch, a blazer, come in and Jake ducks out of the way like it was a high, fast ball which it wasn't. The ball comes right down the pipe and the catcher for the Black Sox purposely misses it. The ball hits Drury right in the chest protector. You hear this 'Woooom!!' Drury goes down like somebody shot him. He actually thought somebody had shot him.

"Jake is laying on the ground laughing. Then he is jumping up and down. Then the players gather around and they are all hollering, 'Are you alright Drury?' It took five minutes before Drury could pull himself back together. Then, Drury threatened to kill Powell. He took off his mask and tried to hit Powell in the face with it.

"Finally, things settled down. A guy came over and pumped up the chest protector so Drury could continue the game."

Pay Day

The teams played a double header every Sunday afternoon for one admission ticket. One side of the stands was for blacks and one side was for whites. That's the way it was in those days . . . totally segregated. Bugle Field could seat about six or seven thousand. The late Roger Pippen, who was the editor for the *Baltimore News Post*, was the paymaster. Charley would guard the door to the little payroll office after the double header when Pippen would dole out the pay to the players.

What Are The Odds

At times, Eckman "earned" additional change thanks to Bugle Field.

Eckman: "A fellow named Elmer Benswanger owned a farm alongside of Bugle Field. He had a big crap game underneath the trestle of the railroad that crossed there. He had a ton of people who would join in this crap game. Us kids would be on

Umpire Eckman at work in the 2nd U.S. Army playoffs, Ft. Meade, MD.

the look out in case the police happened to ride down that far. We would be hollering and Benswanger would break up the game. He walked with a crutch because he only had one leg. Mr. Benswanger, he was a pistol.

He let us kids chase the foul balls during night games at Bugle Field. We would hide them in the ground and mark the area with a tin can. The next morning, we would pull up the tin cans and get a couple baseballs to play with. We always had those baseballs. Many times we would sell them to the teams up around Oliver Street like the Graystones or the Miltons."

Barnstormers

Bugle Field got as much action as an Atlantic City casino buffet when the buses come rolling in. Kept in excellent shape and sporting lights for night games, Bugle Field was a magnet for traveling and semi-pro teams when they had enough money to pay for the lights being turned on. It was also a magnet for young Mr. Eckman even when the Black Sox weren't playing.

Eckman: "The New York Bloomer Girls were a team of women, and I think Babe Dickerson had played with them for a while. They came to Bugle Field to play baseball exhibitions against mens' teams. They had a male pitcher and a male catcher and one male in the infield and maybe another male with the team somewhere. It was four men and five girls and they would tour the country after the season was over to play semi-pro teams throughout the United States. The Bloomer Girls were a pretty good ball club. A couple of those ladies could really hit.

"The House of David had a team that barnstormed too. All the guys had these long beards and they looked like they were students at a rabbinical college. They would play either the Black Sox or semi-pro teams in Baltimore.

"The Silver Moons were a black team that played once a week out at Bugle Field. When the Silver Moons played, the guys would all contribute some money to pay for the lights. I think it cost $35 a night. The Silver Moons team was the best black semi-pro team in Baltimore and they would play the white teams once a week at Bugle Field during the '30s."

In the winter, Bugle Field was the football home to Morgan State, a black college that produced some top pro football players. The Morgan Bears would play under the lights. They had a great athletic director and coach for years and years, Ed Hurt. Charley got a little exercise in when Morgan State played at Bugle Field.

Eckman: "The kickers would kick them field goals and extra points through the uprights, over the fence and out into Loney's Lane. A lot of games were played at night and they used white footballs. I would be in the street with a bunch of other kids and we would grab those footballs when they would come a flyin' and we would start runnin' away with the ball. Now, here comes these guys with the team chasing after us to get the footballs back. We would run up and down Loney's Lane with these guys chasin' after us. We would run, pass the ball and keep running. That's how we got the footballs to play with in the winter."

But Bugle Field was only one of the diamond facets for young Mr. Eckman.

Chapter

18

Diamond Dust

"One of the Cuban players who played for Salisbury told Cambria about this pitcher named Fidel Castro. Cammelas thought Castro was a pretty good pitcher. Cambria brought Castro over for a try out on the Eastern Shore of Maryland."
—*Charles Markwood Eckman, Jr., Bat Boy*

Just Suppose Fidel Castro had Become a Pitcher
in the American Major Leagues . . .

Cambria scouted . . . er . . . mined Cuba for baseball players. He brought a lot of players into organized baseball in the United States. A number of his players made it to the "Big Show." Cambria put together some terrific teams. As an example, Eckman remembers that one year the Salisbury Senators had 38 games taken away from them during one season because of an ineligible player. The team had been in first place by 17 or 18 games. The Salisbury team started over again with no wins and only 60 games left to play in a 100 game schedule and ended up winning about 58 of the 60 games. The key to the team's success was the Cuban players Cambria was bringing in. The Eastern Shore League had teams in Pocomoke, Crisfield, Federalsburg and more.

Eckman remembers Enrico Morales, an outfielder, who knew very little English, but who could run and run and run. He wound up with a team in Omaha, Nebraska. According to Eckman, third baseman, Bobby Estelella made it to the Washington Senators.

Eckman: "He was a little bowlegged guy with a burly chest. He threw rockets across the infield, but he couldn't hit the breaking pitch. As a fielder . . . he would stop them with his chest, his head, his chin, and then pick up the ball and swoosh! He let the ball go and he would holler, 'Hot Mama! Go to Hell!'

"Cambria would keep bringing in these Cuban baseball players. He used to put them up at the Abbey Hotel in Baltimore. 'Moke' Murphy and 'Poke' Whalen would let me go with them when they picked up these ball players arriving in Baltimore. Murphy was a former ballplayer around town, a good hitter. He was the general manager of the Salisbury team. 'Poke' had been a former catcher with the Orioles. Traveling with these men was pretty wild. 'Poke' couldn't drive. He would just sit there and make these snide, funny remarks.

"Cambria got a lot of mileage out of these Cuban players and the Salisbury team wound up with players like George Cammelas and Mike Guerra. Cambria would hold a try out camp and . . . Bingo! Here come some more Cubans.

"One of the Cuban players who played for Salisbury told Cambria about this pitcher named Fidel Castro. Cammelas thought Castro was a pretty good pitcher. Cambria brought Castro over for a try out on the Eastern Shore of Maryland.

"Now, I'm a kid sitting in the back seat of this Chevrolet riding down to the Eastern Shore with Jack Flowers who ran the Salisbury ball club. Flowers had been a third baseman in the Cardinal organization for years. We used to get on the ferry and ride across the Bay and down the road to Salisbury. Well, we get down there and they have a try out camp and Fidel Castro showed that he was a pretty good pitcher with a nifty curve ball.

"Castro wants a hundred and a quarter a month. Cambria and his staff have a big meeting and Joe offers him ninety-five dollars a month. Castro is adamant, but Joe Cambria wouldn't give him another thirty dollars a month. Castro gets mad and goes back to Cuba.

"Years later, Cambria decides to move to Cuba where he is the scout for the Washington Senators. He sold the Bugle Coat and Apron Company on Chester Street in Baltimore and his ball clubs. Joe is signing players and sending them over to the Senators, owned by Clark Griffith, a very thrifty owner. Joe uses all his money to buy property in Cuba.

"The revolution comes with Castro as the head man. He takes everything that Joe Cambria owns . . . confiscated it and threw his ass out of the country. Joe came back to Baltimore a broke man. He lost millions. What would have happened if Cambria gave Castro a hundred and a quarter a month?

"Cambria died broke. A lot of people who knew Joe chipped in to bury him, including myself. The funeral was held at Tickner's Funeral Home, on North and Pennsylvania Avenues. The guys who helped bury him were a who's who in Baltimore sports. Herb Armstrong, the Orioles' long-time general manager and a former coach at McDonough School and a great guy; Tommy Thomas, the former manager of the International League Orioles; Johnny Neun, who had an unassisted triple play in the major leagues when he played for the Detroit Tigers; Congressman Ed Garmatz; and Matt Reinholt, who ran the Bugle Field, were some of those I remember helping to bury Cambria."

Down on Cambria's Farm

The New York State Albany Senators were in the International League in 1933 through 1936. Cambria had pulled together a terrific team.

Eckman: "Jake Powell played center field and went up with the Yankees. There was Fred Sington, from Alabama, who was a former great football player, in left field. He could hit, but he played a fly ball like it was a flying snake. Rupert Thompson went with the Braves. Cy Blanton went with the Pittsburgh Pirates. Ed Chapman, a pitcher, went with the Washington Senators.

"They had a one-eyed first baseman named Del Bissonette. He had formerly played with the old Baltimore Orioles, went up to the big leagues and was back in the minors. They had two good third basemen, Bill Brubaker and Stanley Hack, who was with the Cubs for years. The catchers were Tommy Padden and Hal Finney. Finney would have been a great big league catcher but he lost an arm in an accident with a thrashing machine in Kansas.

Frankie Hayes, of the Athletics, also played there for a while.

"In those days, the major leagues did not have farm teams. They bought players from the minor league owners."

The Pitts from Alabama

Always a promoter, Cambria imported a player from "Sing-Sing," the famous prison. Cambria heard about this convict who earned a reputation as a good running centerfielder for the "Sing-Sing" prison team. His name was "Alabama" Pitts. Cambria figures that having a convict play for the Albany team would be a draw. After all, former prisoners didn't play professional baseball as a rule.

Eckman: "Sure enough, the Senators open the season against Baltimore before a packed house. Pitts opens in center field. Now, Pitts had only played baseball in prison. He had never

1954 Major League Baseball All Star game in Baltimore. Charley, for a change, wasn't the object of photographers' affection. Charley is two rows back and slightly left of Richard Nixon, who is throwing out the first pitch.

played anyplace else, so who knew how good he really was.

"I look around and here comes Pitts ready to bat. I thought to myself here I am with a convict . . . it scared the hell out of me. He threw side arm and hit about the same way you can imagine a side arm throwing centerfielder would hit.

"The first time Pitts threw the ball sidearm, the guys in the dugout all went 'What in the hell is that?!' The ball looked liked a hand grenade coming in or a wounded duck. The rest of the team were laughing and jumping up and down in the dugout. One of the guys hollered, 'He throws like a girl!' Another said, 'What do you expect? He's been in jail for ten years!' They were all having fun at Pitts expense, but not in front of him. When he came into the dugout, they all shut-up.

"He got one single during the day and I liked the guy, a hard-nose fellow. They told me later on that he got killed in a knife fight."

The Harrisburg Follies

The Harrisburg Senators played in the New York Penn League. They were a colorful lot. They played teams from Scranton, Binghamton, Reading, and Hazleton.

Eckman: "Let me tell you how Joe Cambria hired his Harrisburg team Manager in the early Thirties. Cambria was coming out of this minor league meeting and he spots Art Shires lying drunk in the gutter. Shires was a big league ballplayer with the Chicago White Sox, a big league fighter and a big league drinker. They used to call him Arthur 'The Great' Shires. Cambria decided to give Shires a break and let him manage the Harrisburg team.

"Joe Cambria would drive up to Harrisburg at night. I had nothing to do as a kid and I would ride with Cambria to keep him company. Harrisburg had a first baseman named Ed Remorenko, from West Chester State Teachers College. He was a big guy, about 6'3" or 4", and he could hit the ball a ton when he hit it. Once against the Orioles, when he was with Albany, he walloped a ball over the center fielder's head to the scoreboard on one bounce. He ran it into a single . . . which tells you about his power and how fast he could run.

"One night, Remorenko is playing first base against Scranton in the Harrisburg Island ballpark. Harrisburg is ahead two to one. The bases are loaded in the top of the ninth inning with one out. A ground ball is hit to first base. A routine ground ball which should have been a double play and the game is over.

"Remorenko, a left-handed first baseman, comes in to scoop it up. As he goes to get the ball, his spikes get caught in the webbing of his glove and he goes ass over tea cups. The ball goes into right field and he can't get his foot out of his glove. He is rolling all around the field trying to get his foot out of his glove.

"Manager Art Shires was not known for his politeness. He was a very tough guy. As the tying and what proved to be the winning run came flying around the bases, Shires comes out of the dugout with a fungo stick . . . he is trying to hit Remorenko in the head with it. Shires is hollerin', 'I'll kill the son of a bitch . . . let me hit him just once . . . I'll kill him.'

"It took the umpires and the ballplayers to hold Art back. Here's Shires screaming. Remorenko rolling around on the ground and the runners are running and everybody was laughin'. It's was a circus.

"Shires wrecked the clubhouse . . . he wrecked everything he could get a hold of . . . and if he would have got a hold of Remorenko, he would have wrecked him. Arthur 'The Great' Shires was released shortly after that incident."

In a League of Their Own

Maryland has produced a number of Hall of Fame Baseball professionals. George Herman "Babe" Ruth and "Lefty" Grove to name two. But while these gentlemen lived to enjoy their fame, two other baseball greats with Maryland connections did not. Eckman knew both. One was Jimmy Foxx, from Sudlersville, Maryland. Another baseball great, Hack Wilson, born in West Virginia, fell victim to the bottle and died in Baltimore.

The Tom Hanks character in the movie hit *League of Their Own*, about the female league formed in the Midwest during World War II, bears a strong resemblance, in part, to Jimmy Foxx.

Eckman: "In 1954 when I started coaching the Pistons, the first guy I met in the Van Orman Hotel was Jimmy Foxx. I had known Jimmy from Baltimore. He was managing an all-female team in Fort Wayne. Jimmy was pretty much out of it because of his drinking. He was still a big name in the sports world and his name had some marquee value.

"When I was younger, I used to see Jimmy Foxx all the time in Augie Schroll's tavern on Eastern Avenue across from Patterson Park in Baltimore. Schroll was a cop who opened a tavern after he quit the police force. A lot of cops hung out at the place including George Klemmick, a captain in the Homicide Division. He would go over there and with Foxx and a bunch of other guys would sing barbershop harmony half the night. Foxx would be there all night. Klemmick and Foxx were battery mates in the Eastern Shore League. Klemmick was a pretty nifty pitcher coming out of high school into the pros and Foxx was his catcher. Klemmick came up with a bad arm and joined the police force and Foxx went on to the Baseball Hall of Fame.

"Jimmy was a great hitter but he just drank himself out of everything. He died penniless. I was sorry to see it because I liked Jimmy Foxx. I knew his brother, too. Jimmy's brother used to pass himself off as Jimmy and write bad checks. Jimmy would pay them off."

Hack Wilson was another great hitter. He led the National League in home runs and challenged Babe Ruth's record of 60 homers in a year. Hack wound up in Baltimore, but booze brought him down, too.

Eckman: "Wilson died a pauper in Baltimore. Near the end of his life, he was a grounds keeper at Druid Hill Park, one of the largest in the East. He hit 58 home runs in one year in the National League and led the league in hitting and RBIs.

"The amazing thing is he was a little guy, about 5'5" or 6" at the most . . . but, he had big wrists. His wrists looked like they were telephone poles . . . and he would just snap that bat and the ball would jump out of the park."

Eckman, The Baseball Bird Dog

Charley was a part-time scout or "bird dog" for the Philadelphia Phillies under former basketball referee Jocko Collins for 12 years. After the Phillies, he scouted for the Milwaukee Braves for four years for

Honey Russell, another basketball old pal. Eckman: "I was a scout for the Phillies but the big one got away."

In the fifties, major league baseball didn't have a draft. The kids coming out of high school or college were free agents permitted to sign with any team. Major league teams would spend a ton of money trying to out bid each other for these untried phenoms. To bring some sanity to the process, a rule was instituted that if a team gave a bonus over $6,000 to a free agent, the major league team had to keep him on the roster for the whole season.

It was one thing to sign a kid for big bucks and send him out for seasoning, but another to keep him on your roster for a whole year instead of a ball player who could really help you.

Eckman: "I thought that a skinny outfielder playing for Southern High School, in Baltimore, had a ton of potential . . . and I really pushed for the Phillies to sign him. The brass in Philadelphia wasn't as convinced as I was that Al Kaline would make it. Finally, they agreed if Al would sign for less than a six grand bonus that would have kept him on the major league roster for a year.

"I'm the only scout for the Phillies who thought Kaline could play in the major leagues. Now, I'm down with Al and I'm with his family and I've got him convinced to go to the Phillies for a $5,000 bonus.

"But Charlie Gehringer, the General Manager of the Detroit Tigers, saw Kaline play in a high school All Star game in Yankee Stadium, New York. He told his scout, Ed Katalinas, to sign Kaline—period!

"At the last minute, Detroit comes in and signs him for over-the-bonus limit. And the rest, as they say, is history. Kaline stayed on the Detroit major league roster and had a very respectable year for a rookie with no minor league experience. He became a Most Valuable Player in the American League and he is in the Hall of Fame. Katalinas really didn't like Kaline that much but he got credit for signing him.

"Now, here's the kicker. I get a call from the owner of the Phillies, Bob Carpenter. He wants to have lunch. He says to me, 'You're the scout who wanted to sign Al Kaline?' I said , 'Yes, Sir.' He says, 'I'm going to give you an increase in your salary.' Can you believe that? I got a $5,000 a year pay raise for not signing a guy. Eddie Sawyer, a former manager of the Phillies, liked to tell that story at those rubber chicken banquets."

Eckman's role in the resurgence of minor league baseball in Maryland was recognized by Terry L. Randall, who is president of Sports and Recreation Associates, whose organization brought the Frederick Keys to the state. Randall wrote Eckman after receiving the 1992 Baseball America calendar of "Great Minor League Baseball Parks."

The new Harry Grove Stadium in Frederick was featured on the cover of the 1992 Baseball America calendar that highlighted photos of great minor league parks. In his letter Randall wrote, "All too often as we hurry through projects in life, those who provide the initial spark are not properly recognized. Please, be assured that I have not forgotten the man who called me during the summer of 1988 and came to Hagerstown to find out how he could move the discussion of AA baseball in Maryland and baseball in Frederick off of dead-center.

"I have not forgotten who arranged the meeting with Governor Schaefer that started the funding process for the stadium. Charley, it would not have happened without you. I can not begin to thank you enough, and I'm certain that each of the approximately 600,000 fans who have watched games at Harry Grove Stadium would want to shake your hand if I could ever adequately explain the major—but unheralded, role you had in the process."

Eckman was a master of the rubber chicken circuit. Given the number of dinners, banquets and meetings, he addressed as guest speaker, it's a wonder he wasn't on Chicken King Frank Perdue's payroll.

Chapter

19

Never at a Loss for Words

"Here we are at this big meeting of the Southeastern Conference honchos . . . Athletic Directors, football coaches and the like. Speaker after speaker gets up to impart words of wisdom and these dummies ain't listenin', they're boozin' and talkin'. I'm suppose to be the principal speaker and I'm so pissed that I'm ready to give back the fee and go home.

" . . . I decided the money was too good to give back, but, I was determined to get them to shut up. After they introduced me, I got up and shouted into the mike. 'Football players are queers . . . the game is loaded with queers.'

"Well, you could have heard a pin drop. These loud-mouth SOBs stopped, turned around and looked at me. I said, 'I'm a referee . . . a trained observer. I see what's going on on that field. The center gets down and sticks his ass up in the air. He's got a towel covering his butt. Now, the quarterback gets right up behind him, wipes his hands on that towel, flips up that little towel, and puts his hands right under the center's ass. Now, I don't know what the quarterback's pullin' out of there . . . and I don't want to know!' From them on in I had their attention."

—Charles Markwood Eckman, Jr., After Dinner Speaker

Eckman claims that "an expert is a guy from out of town." He became an authority on more than one occasion as a much sought after, and a very funny, after dinner speaker. He appreciated those out-of-town gigs because he was paid in real money. He complained that too often his local speaking engagements resulted in payment in cigars. He received so much tobacco through the years, he could have bought the Phillip Morris Company. Given the current state of that tobacco industry, he opted not to trade those cigars but to smoke them . . . an addiction he never lost.

As a speaker, Eckman gauges his crowd and lets loose with his stories befitting the assembled. Letting loose takes on a much different meaning before a stag group than before a group of nuns.

The reviews of his speaking engagements are a mirror of his officiating and broadcasting careers.

Wilton Garrison, Observer *Sports Editor, of the* Charlotte Observer: "Charlie was equal to the occasion. When it came his turn to speak, he said: 'I'd like to say I'm lost for words, but I'm not,' and proceeded to talk for 40 minutes."

John Steadman, Sports Editor, Baltimore News Post *(American), once wrote:* "Charles Eckman, the man who set the national sports world on its ear by proving that he is a great coach as well as referee, has done it again. Last night he entertained, entranced and generally amused a goodly gathering of folks who went home singing his oratorical praises.

1960 speaking engagement with Coach Honey Russell (Seton Hall).

"To make it even greater, Charlie managed to leave them laughing and impressed all at the same time."

Jack Cruise in a March 1979 report in the New London, Connecticut newspaper, The Day, reported, "Young basketball officials waiting in the wings for their chance got words of encouragement Thursday night from a man who spent 38 years as an official on the high school, college and professional levels.

"Charlie Eckman, speaking at the annual dinner of the Eastern Connecticut Board of Approved Basketball Officials, addressed himself to the young members of the board when he said 'hang in there, don't get discouraged. Your group has the best shot at today's game. You're young and hungry, and you can take a lot of the abuse which goes with officiating today.'

"Eckman told the officials there's no blueprint for officiating, 'Be a salesman when you make a call. Make them (the players) think they made the foul . . . .'

" . . . Outgoing president George Dropo of Plainfield introduced Eckman, a man he said he had met in New York years ago and couldn't wait for the day he got him to speak at a board meeting."

Morris Frank, Philadelphia Inquirer: Bells are ringing in Philadelphia. The Liberty Bell, of course, . . .

"What a lineup of celebs they had—baseball immortals Sandy Koufax, Elston Howard and others, including the colorful and capable Phillies' pilot, Gene Mauch, personable basketball coach Dolph Schayes of the 76ers . . . Football coaches such as the likable Allie Sherman of the Giants and the erudite and witty Dave Nelson of unbeaten Delaware . . .

"National champ jockey Walter Blum. Middleweight champ 'Mr.' Joey Giardello (I call him Mr.) Guess, though, who got the laugh of the night midst all the heros. The popular (yes, popular) basketball Blind Tom, Charley Eckman. The hilarious Charley received applause far louder than any whistle he ever blew."

Bill Evans in his Sports Talk Column covered Charley's speaking engagement in West Virginia:

"Charles Markwood Eckman was a notable choice for the principal speaker when the Northern West Virginia Board of Approved Basketball Officials held its annual soiree for area coaches and other free-loaders in Clarksburg Saturday night. He not only, as they say in show business 'had them rolling in the aisles' with his inimitable stories of his experiences as an official and professional coach, but contributed some sound advice to his fellow whistletooters . . .

"Before he got up to make his 'formal' address, Eckman was presented with an ivory and gold master official's whistle by Stewart Paxton, the former Clarksburger who is now executive secretary of the International Association of Approved Basketball Officials . . .

" 'It'll just fit my big mouth,' quipped Charlie" . . .

Ike Gellis, Sports Editor of the New York Post *wrote:* "Charlie Eckman continues to amaze. His feats on the baseball and basketball field have been told and re-told so the perpetual man in motion came up last night with a new one—oratory. His amusing stories, serious message and great delivery all combined to make it an evening that will be long remembered by the several hundred people who were lucky enough to be on hand."

Millard Tawes, when he was Governor of the State of Maryland wrote: "He perhaps is best known in the world of sports but Judge (Anne Arundel County Orphans Court) Charles Eckman is leaving his mark in a completely different field in Maryland. His wonderful talks to the people in this area have done much to make better citizens of young and old. He is one of our greatest forces for good."

Here Comes the Judge

The first article brilliant sports writer Frank Deford wrote for *Sport's Illustrated* was on Eckman. In it he said: "Eckman helps pay the bills with public relations work and as a much sought-after banquet speaker.

"In the past, his most famous other job came when NBA Referee Eckman was suddenly made NBA coach of the Fort Wayne Pistons. During three full seasons he led the team to two divisional championships and was once named Coach of the Year. He has also played minor-league baseball, umpired minor-league baseball, scouted, dispatched buses, run a pool hall, been a recreation director, a tax investigator ('that's a beauty, ain't it?-referee, umpire and collect taxes in the same year?'), a columnist, a sports commentator, a deputy sheriff and a full-fledged judge of the 'Innurunnle' Orphans' Court.

"The last was a political plum from Maryland Governor Millard Tawes and was supposedly an interim appointment until Eckman would become Secretary of the Racing Commission which he had been more or less supporting over the years, anyway, at the mutual windows. When the commission job went to someone else, Eckman called the governor

Turning the tables: Eckman was roasted three times. Here, with State Comptroller Louis Goldstein (L) and AP Sports Writer Gordon Beard (R).

'a doublecrosser,' and handed in his robes.

"As judge, though, Eckman had left his mark. He is, graciously by his own admission, 'not a grammarian,' but he was never at a loss when a lawyer was foolish enough to start using legal terminology that the Judge was not exactly up on. Judge Eckman simply recessed the court, retired to his chambers, called a lawyer friend who filled him in, and returned to his court. His more heralded verdict, in the tradition of Solomon, concerned a particular will ('Orphans' Court ain't orphans,' explains Charley; 'it is all about wills') being contested by three siblings: two sons who had done no more for their deceased father than take him for a drive occasionally, and one daughter, who had attended the old man faithfully. Arguments over, Judge Eckman banged his gavel. 'You get it all,' he told the daughter. 'I object,' screamed one of the sons. 'The law says I should get one-third.'

" 'All right,' replied Judge Eckman coolly. 'You will. You get one-third of what she don't want. Case closed.'"

Still Holding Court and Making Judgment Calls

Baltimore Sun columnist Mike Olesker has frequently captured the essential Eckman. In this column, he perfectly caught Eckman holding court and making judgment calls: "Charlie Eckman is ad-libbing his way through a noontime in Little Italy with all the subtlety of brass bands.

"Lunching at Sabatino's, waving a cigar like a man orchestrating his own monologue, Eckman is pausing between episodes in what is laughingly called his 'retirement': doing TV commercials for seven different companies, hosting a World Series of Handicapping at two out-of-state racetracks, lecturing here and there, raising decibel levels everywhere, serving as consultant to the governor of Maryland on sports.

" 'Yeah, the governor' Eckman says now, referring to William Donald Schaefer in a voice not unlike an MTA bus backfiring over the 41st Street Bridge. 'The only reason Schaefer is governor and I'm not is City College.'

"The two were classmates there some years back, along with someone named Abe Helfand, who apparently studied.

" 'That's the only reason Schaefer's governor instead of me,' Eckman says again, in case somebody on Fawn Street missed it the first time. 'Schaefer could see Abe Helfand's test paper and I couldn't. He had better eyesight, that's all. He gets the A, and I wind up going to the racetrack.'

" 'Speaking of which,' says a guy across the lunch table, 'why don't you get me a Pimlico pass?' 'Cause you're a gangster,' Eckman says reasonably enough.

"Around the table everybody laughs. Eckman carries a good time into a room. After a few decades of coaching and a few decades refereeing and a few decades broadcasting sports, he says he's been discovered like a brand new debutante . . .

"Two years ago, at 65, he retired from his daily sportscasting at WFBR radio. Married to the same saintly (she'd have to be) woman for four decades. He's the father of four, grandfather of three, and will become a great-grandfather this spring . . . .

"Shy, he never was. Quiet, he never was. Retiring, he never could be."

Despite the offers to go elsewhere for the big bucks, Charley always opted to stay home. It was with great fondness that he remembers the greats and near greats in his home town. Of course, he passes judgment on them, and some people pass judgement on Charley.

Chapter

20

Call A Cab

"Call a cab" is the expression Charley uses when he dismisses a yahoo, a yo-yo or a know-nothing who thinks he knows it all. Along with "It's a very simple game," phrases such as "Better than the movies" and others in his personal lexicon helped define Eckman's persona. That persona has attracted attention in publications local and national in scope. His style as a referee, as a coach, and as a sportscaster has been debated in print through the years like the rings in a cross section of the trunk of a tree . . . an old tree. What others thought of him or revealed about him demonstrates that Charley did not change even though the venues did.

From the Frank Deford *Sports Illustrated* article: "HERE COMES CHOLLY BOP DE BOP BOP . . . the boys were whooping it up in Frank's Den in Glen Burnie, Md. the other night when the door flew open and Charley Eckman bopped in. 'Bop-de-bop-bop,' and other things, Charley yelled to Corky behind the bar and to everyone in front of it. Charley knew everyone in the place. 'Cholly,' asked Dave Spangle, 'do you always got to come on like Gangbusters?' 'If I don't,' Charley said, 'people think I am sick. I walk into the bank or Robinson's Department Store, and if I ain't the boomer, people say, 'Cholly, what is wrong with you?'

"Eckman's bluntness is no act. He is almost pathological on the subject of phonies. Most of them he lumps with the yo-yos. (A yo-yo is 'a guy who goes up and down but don't go nowhere.') . . ."

In another *Sports Illustrated* article on referees, umpires and other officials in 1976, Deford wrote, "Eckman ad-libs all his material, obliterates the English language and makes no bones of the fact that he spends most of his days at racetracks and most of his nights in saloons.

" 'Life's like basketball, better 'n a movie,' Cholly said at the track the other day. 'If you kick one, admit it and keep moving. Wherever you go, Leader, loosen 'em up right away. When I was reffing, the first thing I wanted was to let 'em all know I was going to be there all night, and they weren't going nowheres without me. Then we had some fun. Let's go first class and have some fun, Leader. First class. First class. I like just to sit down in them big seats in front of the plane and watch all them yo-yos go by back to that cave. My wife Wilma says, 'You used to work for a living.' But what's it cost to say hello, Leader, how ya doin', Coach,' Loosen 'em up, Leader.' He bought another Scotch and wheeled the four horse.

"Not long ago, cherry lights on police cars lit up all over Baltimore. Apparently, a bank robbery was in progress in the middle of the night. Actually, Eckman and one of his sponsors were filming a commercial about their new convenient plastic bank cards. Pistols drawn, the first policemen arrived at the bank in their cruiser and saw Eckman standing in the glare of the TV lights. An officer picked up his mike and, in his best Balleemore accent, called in, " 'Hey now, it ain't no robb'ry. It's just Cholly Eckman down here playin'wid his card.'"

Eckman was news where ever he roamed. In 1990, the *Detroit News* published a feature article on Charley.

"It was as a referee that Eckman encountered Jack McCloskey, now the Pistons General Manager and Chuck Daly, now working the bench in the job Charley used to have. 'Jack was a gem at Penn,' Eckman said. Eckman recalled that McCloskey yelled a lot. 'I remember he was coaching Penn, and Bones McKinney was coach at Wake Forest,' Eckman said, 'and they'd pass each other on the floor yelling offense or defense to their teams . . . pass so they'd be at the other team's bench.

" 'I knew Daly when he was an assistant at Duke,' Eckman said. He worked for a guy named Vic Bubas. Daly was more laid-back then. He's gotten more vociferous.'

"One thing about Charley Eckman, bantam, tough, carousing, cigar-chomping: He has not toned down his language over the years. Profane words pour from his mouth; anecdotes are related in a machine-gun staccato.

"Eckman is retired now. He had been working as a sportscaster in

Baltimore Club has Man of the Month, Charley, arrested for charity.
(Photo by Frank DiGennaro.)

Baltimore. He still is deeply involved in banquet speaking, spinning off yarns that are off-color and irreverent. Charley expressed his disdain for another coach turn sportscaster. 'What's he know? He couldn't teach a dog to bark. He says, 'I'm gonna coach the pros.' You don't coach pros. You manage pros. They know how to dribble.'

" 'I had one play. An out-of-bounds play. Plays, the only time they work is on a board. Such a phony thing. What's the guy on defense going to do? Let you run it?' Then a bit of the old referee appeared. 'If they ever call traveling, it'll be a horsebleep league,' Eckman said. 'They take flying steps. The pivot is like a wrestling match.

" 'As a coach,' Charley said, 'I didn't have any clubhouse lawyers.' 'You had Walter Dukes,' he was reminded. Dukes claimed to have gone to law school and supposedly was an actual lawyer. 'He posed as one,' said Eckman. 'Ten years later I found out he didn't have a degree. He was 7-1. Who's going to argue?'. . ."

Eckman's coaching philosophy was reported by Charley Young, Sports Editor of *Buffalo Evening News*, "Charley Eckman, the perpetual sound and motion man who gained fame as a pro basketball coach and referee has a system for beating any team with a superstar in the lineup. Take Wilt Chamberlain for instance. Charley's strategy is quite simple: 'Let him go . . . Don't bother to defense him at all . . . So what if he scores 60 points? How many games can you win with 60 points? Not many. You just let the big star go—a guy like Chamberlain or an Elgin Baylor—and, just guard the devil out of the other four guys.'"

New York University Basketball Coach Don Newbery got to know Charley while serving as the Athletic Director, baseball and basketball coach at the University of Baltimore (U. of B.) from 1958 to 1961. After a conversation with Charley, Newbery arranged an athletic scholarship for Charley's son, Barry, who played baseball and soccer at the U. of B.. Don served as a basketball coach at NYU from 1961 to 1970.

Newbery was utterly amazed when he bumped into this Maryland referee and umpire for the first time in the Big Apple. He did not realize at the time that New York was Charley's kind of town and had been for years. Both were heading into the entrance for officials and teams at Madison Square Garden where NYU played their home basketball games, when Charley hollered his greeting. As they passed the guard at the gate, another voice rang out, "Hey, Cholly!" Newbery watched Eckman head toward the guy and put his arm around the maintenance worker. Eckman did all the talking and both roared with laughter.

The scene was repeated moments later with an elderly cleaning lady who greeted Charley with glee. More happy talk and the lady departed laughing. Can this be a referee from Baltimore wondered Newbery?

Newbery said that he learned from Charley how important it was to communicate with people, support staff, as well as players, alumni and administrators. He also learned that Eckman was a genuine celebrity in New York and wasn't simply an official from Baltimore.

Newbery recalls the one that got away and Eckman was in the middle of it, but Don wasn't sure what part Charley played. A Pennsylvania high school player, Jay McMillen, older brother of future basketball great and Congressman, Tom McMillen, was the object of Newbery's affection for his NYU team. Young Jay visited the campus of the predominately Jewish school and returned home to announce to his parents that he wanted to go there. Don suspected that Jay was enamored of playing home games in the Garden.

McMillen's mother called Newbery demanding to know what he had done to her son who she emphatically wanted to attend a Catholic College. Newbery invited her see what NYU was all about. He wined and dined her along with the priest of the NYU Catholic Club, put her up at a hotel overnight. The next day, he showed her the campus and she met with officials.

The piece de resistance was the Notre Dame–NYU game, a fierce, rivalry sold out for months in advance. Newbery arranged for seats for Mrs. McMillen and her sister, a Long Island resident, along side of VIP NYU Alumni including the president of the MGM Movie Studio. After the game, won by NYU, Newbery took her and her sister to Mamma Leone's, the legendary New York restaurant.

While having drinks before ordering, Eckman exploded into the place, spotted Newbery and announced to everyone Newbery's celebrity status. Charley invaded the table and asked Newbery why was he there with "two broads." Don explained that weren't "broads" but they were two ladies important to his recruiting effort.

Newbery said that Eckman knew he was paying with recruitment funds and Charley kept ordering and ordering and ordering. They closed Leone's that night and Charley called a cab, herded the trio in to it and closed two more drinking joints before calling it quits. At every stop, Charley was greeted like a long, lost brother. Newbery didn't have a dime of recruiting money left by the end of the evening.

The next thing Newbery knows is that McMillen signs with the University of Maryland. Newbery adds, "I never did find out what happen. Jay's mother wanted him to go to a Catholic College. Jay wanted to come to NYU, but Maryland, in Eckman's home territory, gets him."

When Newbery was in Baltimore, there was one occasion he was overjoyed to see Eckman. Newbery was warned that when his U. of B. baseball team went to play a certain college in the hills of Virginia, his team was sure to lose. He relates that fellow Athletic Directors and baseball coaches had warned him that the local umpires were "Homers" favoring the local college.

He was relieved when he saw a guy in the parking lot pull from his car a chest protector worn by the home plate umpire. The guy was Eckman. As Charley headed to field in his uniform, Don leaned back in the dugout, and told his assistant coaches, "Relax, guys! The only 'homers' today will be the balls that clear the fence between the foul poles." The U. of B. won the game.

Hawk O'Brien, one of Charley's life long friends, played on the same teams as Charley in various leagues including the Baltimore City College High School team. Hawk said that young Charley honestly came by the nickname "Gabby." He added that Eckman, who earned All Maryland honors as a second baseman, drove his high school coach, Ken Van Sant, crazy with his constant talking.

Charley was the lone umpire for a league game in 1948 that pitted the Brown Derby's, O'Brien's team, against the Shrine of the Little Flower Church team at Herring Run Park. With Hawk on second base, a hitter slashed a grounder through the right side of the diamond. Hawk cut off third base to score standing up. His buddy Eckman, the umpire, called him out for missing third base. Hawk went nose to nose with Charley and said, "I saw you follow that ball in to the outfield. There's no way you saw me comin' around third." Charley replied, "O'Brien, you ain't that fast! There ain't no way you can score from second if you touched third base. You're out and you can go to sleep on them cherries!"

Hyman Cohen, prominent Baltimore attorney and a long supporter of theatrical arts, fondly remembers Charley from their Baltimore City College days. Sixteen year old Hy was a sophomore manager of the baseball team. He said Charley took him under his wing and always walked with him to practice in Clifton Park. He added that every time Coach Van Sant would send him out to buy chewing gum for the team before a game, Eckman was first in line to pick out his favorite flavor. Cohen added that Charley not only had Van Sant in a tizzy with his talking, but he drove his teammates crazy too.

Twenty years lapsed before they met again. Cohen was dining in a downtown Baltimore restaurant when Charley boomed into the room and blasted out, "Hey, Hy . . . where's my gum."

When Charley was serving as a Judge of Anne Arundel County Orphan's Court, he recessed a proceeding and called Cohen asking for his opinion on the case Eckman was hearing. Cohen expressed his opinion and gave his reasons. Charley said, "Hey, leader! Thanks for helping me on this one. I don't think you're right," and hung up.

Still more on Eckman, the baseball umpire. In one of his *Baltimore Sun* columns, Dan Rodricks wrote . . . "A Harford County man named N. Joseph Lee Jr. remembered something that happened while Charley umpired a game in the Susquehanna League in the early 1950s. 'Once I was pitching and doing well,' Lee says. 'We had many runs and, if I remember correctly, the other team had none. Late in the game I threw one right down Broadway; it split the plate right across the belt.

Charley called it a ball. I headed for the umpire. With a flourish, Charley removed his mask and chest protector and met me in front of the plate. I don't remember exactly what I said but it was probably, 'You blind bum, what was wrong with that one?' His reply: 'Nothin', I just wanted to see what you would say.' "

. . . And Craig Hankin remembers almost driving off a highway when, on the car radio, he heard Charley declare on WFBR that some baseball team owner was "so cheap he wouldn't pay a quarter to see Jesus come back on a bus!"

The "Key" Connection

Harvey Kasoff, who played for the Baltimore City College high school basketball team, relates a referee Eckman "kindness." Charley and Harvey's father, who owned Key Wine and Liquor Company. a distributorship, were good friends. When Harvey was a bench-warming sophomore rookie, he was a mop-up substitute late in a game as City was being blown out by the opposition. Eckman circled the youngster and told him to dribble the ball until he bumped into someone.

Kasoff charged his defender and Eckman gives it the "old federal case" in calling a blocking foul. When the young man who Kasoff plowed into started to protest, Charley stopped him in his tracks and told Kasoff to go to the line for two shots. At the foul line, Charley said under his breath, "Now kid, there ain't no way your team is gonna' win, but I promised your old man that I would help you get into the scoring column in the newspaper. So, take your time and put at least one of these shots in the basket . . . and tell your old man he owes me one."

The relationship with the Kasoff family continued throughout Charley's life. A necessary stay by Charley at St. Agnes hospital in Baltimore illustrates that relationship.

During the last game of the 1969 NFL for the Baltimore Colts against the Rams in Los Angeles, Eckman began feeling uncomfortable during his colorcast duties. The team trainers gave him various stomach settling medicines to ease his discomfort on the flight back to Baltimore.

His doctor discovered the problem was Charley's gall bladder, which had a grander coming out party than most debutantes have ever experienced. After completing my evening shift, including subbing for Charley on the sportscast at WCBM, I went to visit him at hospital. I was concerned that I might not make it in time as I arrived just as visiting hours were coming to the end.

I moved against the flow of people leaving who had come to see their loved ones until I reached the hallway where Eckman's room was located. There the flow had reversed. Doctor's, nurses, and interns coming off duty were enroute to Charley's room.

His room resembled a speakeasy without live music but enough high ranking police officers to constitute a raiding party. Father Neil O'Donnell was tending bar. Father Marty Schwalenberg was holding court. Eckman had the crowd in more stitches than his incision (pun intended) with his twice told tales. Lots of specimen bottles were being filled with high octane stuff that had been aged in charred kegs or grew on corn stalks.

I strongly suspect that the surgeons found and removed a couple of old referee whistles and a bunch of losing tickets from the races at Pimlico in addition to the faulty gall bladder. This was never proven.

The morning after my visit, Charley called me at the radio station, and said, "Leader, call Key Wine and Liquor and tell Harvey to send me up a case of miniatures (liquor). Tell 'em if I stay in this hospital another night, I may need a couple a' more cases."

The Local Angle

As a referee, Eckman was never a "homer" meaning he did not favor the home team. But in real life, he was. His wife, Wilma, his kids, and his friends kept him in his home town despite broadcasting offers in New York, Los Angeles and other cities that would have paid him a six-figure salary.

There is no denying the affection he had for the home folks. Local basketball did not have the glamour of the Atlantic Coast Conference or the National Basketball Association, but Charley worked those games as if they were the most important in the world and he remembers the area greats and the great games. One of the greats was Jim Lacy, a popular Baltimore insurance man who, for many years, held the career record for points scored in a college career.

> Eckman: "Jimmy Lacy was an outstanding shooter, a pure shooter. He could shoot with anybody. One night at Seton Hall, Lacy and Pep Saul, who went on to play with Rochester in the pros, hooked up in one helluv a shooting exhibition. Seton Hall was coached by Bob Davies and Loyola was coached by Lefty Reitz, two fine basketball men.

Charley waves to the gallery as he is honored with a Maryland House of Delegates Resolution. Presenting the award is Speaker of the House Ben Cardin, now a Congressman.

"Saul and Lacy threw in about eight shots in a row each . . . it was a shooting contest. They would take these two-hand sets and they did not miss. Lacy could drive and had a pretty good turn around shot and he could rebound pretty good. He would drive across the key and lay it in. Jimmy was a pure shooter. He could have played in pro ball had he been so inclined. "

Across Maryland and DC

Eckman liked American University, the Washington, D. C. team coached by Stan Cassell. According to Charley, Cassell was an "excellent person and a good coach."

Another guy Eckman had great respect for was Jimmy Phelan, coach of Mount St. Mary's College, in Emmitsburg, Md. Charley claims

Phelan started coaching at Emmitsburg when George Washington was elected president. Phelan coached a lot of outstanding teams. Charley remembers Pete Clark "who could go to the top of the key and to the hoop without stopping. He could jump out of the building."

Eckman also remembers Western Maryland and a player named Art Press who could shoot that two-hand set shot.

> Eckman: "On the Eastern Shore, Tom Kibler was Mr. Washington College. He had Ed Athey coaching the club, nicest guy in the world. And he had a fellow named Nick Scallion, who had a one hand, left-hand jumper. Scallion and Art Press put on a show one night on the Western Maryland campus. They must have scored 28 points a piece. Nobody else on either team shot the ball . . . just those two and they didn't miss. Press with his set shot . . . a New York type ball player, and Scallion who could take a jump shot and hit it, had a great touch around the basket."

Sports columnist Harry S. Russell of the Kent County News, *Chestertown, Maryland remembered Charley officiating on the Eastern Shore of Maryland in a very personal column dated Wednesday, March 29, 1967, titled "Goodbye, Charley!*

"Anyhow, after 29 years, Charley Eckman, one of the best and most colorful whistle-tooters ever to grace a basketball court, has hung up his cage clothes.

"Unless you are a basketball fan, you probably don't know Charley. For years, he officiated in the Mason-Dixon Conference before and after going to the top in the professional NBA. Eckman has officiated many times in Chestertown where he was and is extremely popular.

"Charley's experiences could fill a book—maybe they will some day.

"This department will best recall him as he hot-footed it down the court—walkathon style, seldom a run—glancing in the stands to spot a friend and calling out: 'Hi Russ, see you out to Bud's after.' Maybe he wasn't the most colorful official the game has known but he'll do until something better comes along."

Baltimore Reflections

The NBA in modern times has its share of Baltimore players. Attracted by a chance to escape from the Inner City and make big bucks, kids play basketball year round in leagues and school. In the '30s and '40s, basketball was still an escape, even if million dollar contracts weren't the lure. Ethnic pride was the driving force. Eckman was on many courts . . . officiating . . . to see it unfold.

Eckman: "Baltimore had a lot of basketball courts filled with action. The recreation center in Hampden was a great place to see games. The best was the Broadway Armory. They had an old sergeant in the National Guard who sat upstairs with a .45 Caliber pistol on his hip. He looked foreboding but he was a good man. He stopped all the fights and the bullcrap that went on. We played down at the Knights of Columbus hall in Highlandtown, on a court on top of the building.

"Back in the 30s, when I refereed in the big time—the Baltimore Basketball League, the best of local basketball—for $7.50 a game . . . that was a lot of money in those days. The best team in town was "Pop" Schuerholz's Arundel Boat Club. Gil Schuerholz was a tremendous athlete and his brother, Johnny, had a deadly set shot. This was a runnin' team.

"The Young Mens' Hebrew Association (YMHA), the Jewish team, was up there as one of the best teams in Baltimore. You had guys like Tommy Reamer who could hit that set shot, 'Hunkie' Matz, whose son Ron has had a long career in radio and TV in Baltimore, 'Snickles' Friedman, 'Bones' Battelion and the others who really knew how to play the game. The best attraction was when YMHA played the Arundel Boat Club. The house was always packed at 40 cents a head.

"When they played at the Fourteen Holy Martyr Court, Father Kelly ran the concession stand. The Jewish guys liked to have a buck or two for a stake on who would win the game and Father Kelly would hold the money. 'Ham' Horowitz, on the YMHA team, use to throw epileptic fits and dive on the floor if his team was losing. About two minutes to play, he would throw a fit and froth at the mouth, and jump around on the floor, and everybody would stop and we would watch him. Father Kelly would pray for him a little bit, and "Ham" would get up and play would resume with everybody getting a second wind. That was the first gambling I ever saw in basketball.

"Max Toy and Bud Skelly played in the Catholic league. Toy was maybe the best passer I ever saw. He could handle the ball with anybody and he later refereed with me.

"The YMCA was fair with Tommy Keller. The Knights of Columbus, they had a pretty good ball club. The Stonewall's, sponsored by a political club, had Marty Hauser, Jimmy Knell, a pretty good shot, and 'Snitz' Snyder, a big center.

"The Klemmick boys, Charlie and George, played for the Baltimore Athletic Club. They were good basketball players as well as good soccer players. Bill Adams ran the league.

"I had a lot of fun with the Susquannocks. Certain rivalries in the league were fierce. Then you had the other teams in the West Baltimore Inter-Club League such as the Gilcos, with Buddy Myers, and Frank Bova who could shoot the ball. They didn't do any one-hand push shots, or go by the basket and throw the hook up from underneath. It was straight, pure, clean basketball in those days."

Soccer, the Number One Sport?

Eckman: "All the soccer players from the Baltimore Soccer Club, guys like Bob Adams, and Jimmy Adams, all played. And they played basketball like they played soccer . . . bang! . . . bop! . . . sock! Nobody did anything much but they had a good time. I played soccer. It was something to do when I had a night off from officiating.

"Soccer was the ruling sport in the winter in Baltimore. All these dummies around town that tell me they don't know anything about soccer, they are full of stuff, because soccer was the big sport in Maryland, especially in Baltimore, in the late 30's prior to World War II. Soccer was the game, and you would have three or four games every Sunday, at Clifton, Patterson, Gwynns Falls, Swann Park, and Carroll Park. In those days, soccer was the game . . . basketball was a necessary evil, and football was unheard of.

"And always in those days the basketball players were goal keepers in soccer because they had good hands, like Bill Southcomb, who played with the Canton Soccer Club and the Baltimore Soccer Club. Gil Schuerholz could play goal or center forward. 'Peck' Ellis was a good goalie and played both sports. Charlie Klemmick was another good goal keeper because of his excellent hands from playing basketball.

"Soccer is great. The players can run around and holler to

the crowds, and we know it's the international sport. Soccer is also the greatest conditioning sport in the world. I played soccer with the kids, until my 50's. I would run up and down the field. I would build my wind up so I could referee basketball. It's a very simple game. Football was not the dominant sport that people want to think it was prior to World War II."

Many years before Charley was involved with indoor professional soccer, he was pushing the outdoor game. Eckman was a great advocate and promoter of soccer. It made no difference at what level, Charley was in there pitching. Before he became the dean of Baltimore area TV sports anchors, Vince Bagli was a writer for the *Baltimore News Post*. He wrote, "Charlie Eckman who never tip-toes anywhere, came thundering into the sports department yesterday and after a snappy salutation for all of the 'wheels,' the word he uses to greet everybody, immediately launched into a wordy discourse on the Pompei Soccer Club.

" 'When we were growing up, soccer was a big thing all over town, 'and there are enough people to draw from in this area to bring the sport back to the popularity it once knew.'"

The Ref Who Stayed a Mailman

Charley developed a friendship with Frank Taneyhill, who played at Loyola and became an official.

Eckman: "Frank refereed with me in the West Baltimore Club League. He was a big guy, about 6'3" or 4" and a fine person. He might have been the best basketball referee in Maryland but he was always scared to leave the Baltimore area. I tried to get Taneyhill to referee pro ball. I used to say, 'Come on Frank, go with me. I will get you in the league.' 'No,' he told me, 'I am going to get a job in the post office as a mail carrier.' He wound up being a mail carrier for years. He was a tremendous person and a great referee and should have gone further."

An Arresting Team on the Local Diamond

One of best amateur baseball teams in Baltimore during the thirties, according to Eckman, was the Baltimore Police Department team. They would play other amateur teams during the week, but on the weekends, the players would scatter to play for top notch semi-pro teams to pick-up $10 to $15 a game. That was a lot of money in those days.

Eckman: "These guys were outstanding ballplayers and they gave any team they played fits. They had a tough group of pitchers like 'Hen' Sherry, 'Buck' Foreman, Bill Runge, Harry Biemiller and others. The catchers were Johnny Alberts, Joe Koenig, and Pete Stack. Around the infield was 'Hobey' Hammen on first . . . Jimmy Lyston at second . . . Eddie Sawyer played short stop . . . Tony Schoehoff on third. Their top back-up infielder was 'Inky' Gueff. Patrolling the outfield (no pun intended) were George Klemmick in center field, with Joe Zukas in left . . . Augie Schroll was in right with Freddy Fitzberger off the bench. The other guys were good but these are the guys that stand out in memory. Sergeant Polly Martin was the manager, but the guy who ran the team was Captain 'Buck' Hartung.

"The Baltimore City Fire Department had a pretty good team too with Buddy Campbell, Bobby Fold in the infield, Harry White in the outfield, and Grayson Standiford on the mound.

"These teams would play a wild series of home and away games against each other and teams from the Norfolk Police Department and the Quantico Marines. I remember the Baltimore Police Department team taking the overnight steamer from downtown Baltimore to Norfolk. A lot of the guys would get so plastered and rowdy on the boat, they would get locked up for their own protection when they got to Norfolk. They sobered up, got out of jail and played ball.

"When I was a kid, everyone knew the cops. Nobody gave the cops lip. The police were respected and it was great for the morale of the Police Department and the public. Those were the days."

The News American, *a Sunday feature on Dec. 15, 1985, by John Hawkins, had a big banner headline with an Eckman caricature.* "Good Time Cholly has done it all, and he'll gladly tell you about it . . . With Baltimore institution Eckman, what you hear is what you get . . . Everybody who walks through the door knows Eckman. He is Baltimore. He is crabs and beer. He is a big mouth with something to say. He is noticeable."

Given Eckman's impact on sports nationally and locally, it is amazing that he has not been elected to the Maryland State Sports Hall of Fame. Pat O'Malley, sports columnist for the Anne Arundel regional edition for the *Baltimore Sun*, campaigned to have that oversight remedied.

Anne Arundel County Sun, *February 20, 1991: O'Malley wrote a column under the headline,* "Eckman, a county treasure, still ignored by Hall of Fame."

"There is something about an obvious injustice that evolves from those who harbor grudges that infuriates me and maybe you, too. So, please allow me, sports fans, to get it off my chest before cranking up my 'Q's without A's' machine today.

"After looking over the credentials of the four people inducted in the Maryland State Athletic Hall of Fame this week, it really bothers me that year after year Glen Burnie's own Charlie Eckman is overlooked.

"The executive secretary of the Hall of Fame Committee . . . says the reason Eckman is kept out is because they don't honor coaches. Did those honored by the Hall perform their Hall of Fame efforts without coaches and officials. Is that why many of the inductees made it, because they were so good they didn't need coaching or guidance? . . .

"This no-coach thing is one way to keep out the man who, for nearly three decades, broadcast the feats of amateur athletes and those who have gone into the Hall.

"Eckman deserves to bask in the glory of what I know would be his biggest moment in sports."

O'Malley's column prompted lots of calls in favor of Charley's induction into the Maryland Sports Hall of Fame. He printed a few including the following:

"Odenton's Dave Owen put it this way: 'I'd be the first one to call that man a cab and take him to the Hall of Fame.'

"Vic Lotterer of Severna Park: "Charlie should have been in there a long time ago and that's what the people want.'

"And 63-year-old Doris Jenkins, who recently was selected as only the second woman ever to be named to the Maryland Softball Hall of Fame: 'I played women's basketball in Baltimore and often watched Charlie referee. He was the most respected referee around in high school, college and even the NBA. As only the second woman to ever go into the Softball Hall of Fame, I understand the bias, prejudice and jealousy that is possibly now confronting Charlie. Get him now while he's still alive.'"

In 1979, Roast-master Eckman with Congress-woman (now U.S. Senator) Barbara Mikulski at East Baltimore Citizens Political Committee event. (Photo by F.A. Matricciani.)

In 1995, Frank Deford lamented on his National Public Radio broadcast that Charley and his student, Mendy Rudolph, had been overlooked by the National Basketball Hall of Fame. Deford hoped that the pair would be inducted for their outstanding contributions to the sport.

Charley had no trouble making it into other sports halls of fame. Eckman was inducted in the Maryland Oldtimer's Baseball Association Hall of Fame, the Maryland Boxing Hall of Fame, and his home county Hall of Fame. *The Maryland Gazette,* October 16, 1991 reported on the induction of Charley Eckman as one of five charter members into the Anne Arundel County Sports Hall of Fame. Writer Bill Wagner called Eckman "sportsman extraordinaire."

Politics—Another Eckman Game

Charley delved in and around politics for years. He ran for public office without success, but injected a lot of fun in the ordinarily dull proceedings. Roy Gregory, of the *Baltimore News American,* interviewed State Senate candidate Eckman for his September 19, 1977 column (severely abridged version):

"Call A Cab, You #*!@& Politicians: Eckman Is Running For State Senate

"RG—What makes you so confident you would make a good senator?

"CE—Are you still kidding? Look at the yo-yo who represented the district. He wheeled and dealed for seven years and wound up grabbing a $38,000-a-year state job. Now, don't go getting me wrong. In politics there has to be wheeling and dealing but a good politician wheels and deals for the people he represents and not for himself. If I couldn't do a better job for my constituents, I would call a cab to take me from Annapolis back to Glen Burnie."

Lights, Camera, Eckman!

In January 1974, Sportscaster Eckman was featured as the *Movie Mirror* magazine Personality of the Month. Years later, Charley had a near brush with movie stardom, the first since his holler guy days in Pathe' movie shorts shortly after WW II.

The making of a movie atrocity known as *Blood Circus* backed by a Maryland based TV jewelry huckster was being filmed in the Baltimore Civic Center, now known as The Arena. The sponsor advertised that some 20 well known wrestlers would be yanking off each others arms, legs and heads and tossing them into the audience. They scheduled two shows and charged $9.95 for admission. Instead of the 12,000 "extras" expected for the first show, only 700 people showed up, proving not everyone in Baltimore is a sucker.

Movie making is a slow business and lousy movie making is even slower, especially when the crowd paid to see blood. When one customer shouted "Give us our money back," Eckman, who was ad libbing his role as the ringmaster anyway (he was a paid performer on this occasion), retorted, "You never had any money to begin with. How can we give it back?"

Life has been a fight for Charley. A fight to make a living for his widowed mother. A fight to obtain more games to referee. A fight to make a living for his family. A fight to become a coach. Charley had to fight for his life.

Eckman battled his colon cancer for years as the Olesker column titled "Call a cab, indeed: Charley Eckman is going home," revealed.

"Charley Eckman, having endured five cancer operations in the past month, including two in one day, and being weak and (as everybody knows) naturally shy and soft-spoken to begin with, is sitting in his room at North Arundel Hospital with his voice turned all the way up.

" 'This ain't what I asked for, is it, hon?' he says, in tones like the tuba section of a marching band. Charley's the only one who ever spent a few decades in broadcasting and never particularly needed a microphone to be heard. Now he's talking about this quart of ice cream his daughter, Gail, has brought him, which he's devouring in its entirety despite it being not quite the right flavor.

"Along with the ice cream, he's had company. His barber, Bobby McGee from Dundalk, dropped in to do a little trim work. His wife, Wilma, is here, plus a stream of visitors that includes his four children, his grandchildren, some sports figures, some old friends. Everybody tiptoes in, looking worried, and then Charley proceeds to hold court for an hour at a clip.

"The doctors told him he's got to take it easy. Charley's got needles and tubes attached to him, various electronic monitors here and there, and nurses checking every few minutes. An entire health industry seems to have been constructed around him.

" 'I thought I was gone the other night,' he says now, 'but then I thought, 'I don't know where it is I'm supposed to go.'

"He's laughing as he says this, but there's truth behind the bravado. It's been a rough time. The doctors fought the colon cancer, then sent him home for a few days last week, but a high fever brought him back for more tests.

" 'When can I go home again?' Eckman asks a doctor. 'We'll see,' the doctor says.

" 'You gotta be more specific than that,' Eckman, 72, barks at him. 'I've lived my whole life by the clock.'

"That, he has. If he wasn't watching the basketball clock, he was racing to pay the bills . . .

"He found a softer gig. Did two decades of radio at a couple of local stations, swaggering his way through several broadcasts a day. Became a kind of cult figure. Invented his own jargon. ('Call a cab.')

"Threw in some TV stuff, occasionally ad-libbing politics along with the sports. Everybody in modern TV history relies on TelePrompters, but not Charlie. He'd scribble a few notes on a matchbook cover, and use them if he needed them.

" 'It's a very simple game,' he's always said, and it never mattered which particular game he was talking about. Always, Charley's brought with him the street guy's disdain for pseudo-sophistication. He's got the subtlety of an uppercut. That's why he told his doctors to give it to him straight: When could he go home? That's why everybody was delighted, yesterday morning, when they told him he could leave today."

More on Charley and the Kids

Eckman's fight against cancer never stopped him from doing what he liked doing best—holding court and helping people. In 1993, State Senator Michael Wagner of the "Take Back Our Streets" organization wrote:

"Dear Charlie,

"I would like to take this opportunity to personally thank you for taking out time from your busy schedule to attend our first annual 'Sports Celebrity Reception'. Your presence made the evening a great success. The incredible turn out we had that night, is a testament to your contribution to the world of sport.

"Thanks to your efforts that evening, our organization was able to raise $19,000 for the Anne Arundel County Police Department's Youth Activities Program. With summer not far off—and the program expanding daily, these funds will go a long way to help a great bunch of kids avoid the temptations of drugs and the downward spiral associated with that life style."

The Good Scout

On January 10th, 1995 the Four River District Boy Scouts honored Charley with his "Good Scout of the Year Award." At that event, Sports Columnist John Steadman said of Charley, "He did not come down from Mount Olympus. He came up from the streets."

Broadcast executive Harry Shriver was quoted as saying that "Charley is an American original."

Then the Lord blew the whistle! The game came to an end. The fight was over.

Epilogue

On July 3, 1995, with the fighting in Bosnia still going on, terrorists attempting to break up the Middle East peace process, AIDS running rampant, and incurable viruses emerging in Africa, the Lord must have wanted a few laughs, or maybe a lot of them. On that day, the booming voice of this extraordinary personality, fell silent. The game of life was over, stilled by colon cancer.

His funeral was attended by the people he loved, a who's who of celebrities from all walks of life, and many he didn't know personally but who loved him because of his broadcasts or wide ranging sports activities that touched their lives.

His family selected just four people of the many who wanted to eulogize him. Sports columnists John Steadman and Pat O'Malley, Baseball Hall of Fame sportscaster Chuck Thompson and batting clean-up, Monsignor Martin Schwalenberg (a Catholic priest in a Presbyterian Church).

Father Marty covered Charley's love for his family. Pat O'Malley talked about Eckman's vernacular language he called "Ecklish".

Steadman recalled the time when a toll booth struck Charley's car in self-defense late one evening. The *Sun* reported the incident in the morning edition. Concerned, Steadman called his friend and asked how he was doing. Charley's reply was, "Why do you ask?" Steadman told him what he read about the incident in the news and he wanted to know if Charley was okay. Charley replied, "There ain't no problem. The monsignor (Schwalenberg) is here now. He said a few prayers. Gave me absolution or something and the slate is clean again."

Thompson said that he could imagine the scene when Charley made it to the heavenly gates and St. Peter was ready to review the Eckman record. Just then the Lord stepped in and said, "I'll handle this. This one is a job for the varsity."

As Charley's mortal remains left the church, a Dixieland band played the happy music that was symbolic to those of us who saw him in action or heard him. Charley wanted it this way. It's a very simple game!

The End

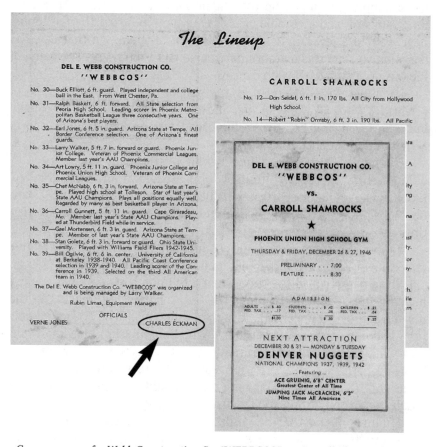

Game program for Webb Construction Co. "WEBBCOS" vs. Carroll Shamrocks, 1946. Charley is listed as an official.

For the Record

Basketball Achievements of Charley Eckman

The following list of achievements by Charley Eckman was compiled by one of foremost basketball journalists in the Unites States, Seymour Smith, a retired Assistant Sports Editor of the *Morning Sun* newspaper. Smith compiled his list for the nomination of Eckman to the Basketball Hall of Fame.

As a Basketball Official

- Officiated professional, collegiate, club and high school basketball for 27 years.
- Officiated in the first NBA East–West All Star game.
- Officiated in two National Collegiate Athletic Association (NCAA) Championship games.
- Officiated in eight National Invitation Tournaments (NIT).
- Officiated in the National Basketball Association (NBA), Atlantic Coast Conference (ACC), Eastern Collegiate Athletic Conference (ECAC or Big East), Ivy League, Mason–Dixon Conference, Southern Conference, National AAU Industrial League, American (West Coast) League, Border (now Southwestern) Conference among others.
- Averaged officiating 80 games a year. During one season, he officiated in 148 games.
- Averaged five tournaments during colleges Christmas break.
- Listed as Dallas Shirley's Number One referee for crucial games. Shirley is a member of the Basketball Hall of Fame. He served as the Chief Official for numerous collegiate basketball conferences and was responsible for assigning referees to officiate games.
- Regarded by many the chief official (Maryland–D.C.)

Typical work week as an official:
Sunday—AAU game
Tuesday—ACC game
Wednesday—Navy or Southern Conference game
Thursday—ECAC or Southern Conference game
Friday—Ivy League
Saturday—ACC, Ivy League, ECAC, or Mason–Dixon Conference

There is more on his coaching career . . .

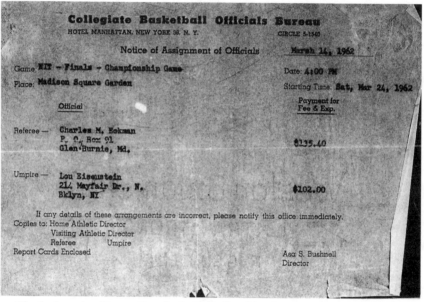

Charley's contract as a college basketball official for the NIT Final Championship Game, Madison Square Garden, Mar 24, 1962.

Coaching Career

In 1954, after serving as a professional basketball official for seven years, the owner of the Fort Wayne Zollner Pistons, Fred Zollner, selected Eckman to replace Paul Birch as coach. In just three and one half years, Eckman accomplished the following:

● NBA Coach of the Year for 1954–55.
● Eckman coached his team to a 43–29 record in 1954–55 for Western Division Championship.
● Eckman coached his team to a 37–35 record in 1955–56 for Western Division Championship.
● Eckman coached his team to a tie for the Western Division Championship in 1956–57.
● The Pistons did not come close to winning a championship for another 32 years.
● Eckman was the only coach between 1954 through 1957 to win more than one championship.
● Eckman was the only coach between 1954 through 1957 to place his team into two NBA title games.
● From 1954 through 1957, Eckman coached the second highest number of victories 114. Red Auerbach of the Celtics, with Bob Cousy and Bill Russell, won 119.
● The 43 win season in 1954–55 was the third best in the 1954 through 1957 period. Philadelphia, under George Senesky, ranked first in the period with 45 wins in the 1955–56 seasons.
● Eckman was the coach of the West All Stars in two NBA All Star games, 1954–55 and 1955–56. He won the 1955–56 game as an underdog.
● Eckman is the only person to have officiated in a NBA All Star game and coach in the NBA All Star game.
● Eckman's use of four "big men" and one guard in the 1955–56 West All Star team victory changed the thinking of coaches in the NBA on the use of "big" guards.
● Eckman was one of the first voices (1960) to suggest the NBA put a premium on baskets made three feet beyond the foul line "key."

The Statistics on the Winningest Coaches in the NBA 1954–1957

Most Victories:
>   Red Auerbach, Celtics 119
>   **Charley Eckman**, Pistons...............114
>   John Kunda, Lakers.........................107

Most Victories Single Season:
>   George Senesky, Warriors 45 (1956)
>   Red Auerbach, Celtics, ...44 (1957)
>   **Charley Eckman**, Pistons...............43 (1955)
>   Al Cervi, Nationals.........................43 (1958)

Most Division Championships:
>   **Charley Eckman**, Pistons ....2 ('55 & '56)
>   Al Cervi, Nationals..........................1 (1955)
>   George Senesky, Warriors..............1 (1956)
>   Red Auerbach, Celtics 1 (1957)
>   Alex Hannum, Bombers.................1 (1957)

Most Times in Championship Playoffs:
>   **Charley Eckman**, Pistons ....2 ('55 & '56)
>   Al Cervi, Nationals..........................1 (1955)
>   George Senesky, Warriors..............1 (1956)
>   Red Auerbach, Celtics 1 (1957)
>   Alex Hannum, Bombers.................1 (1957)

Best Home Record for Western Division team: 62–22

Eckman's 43 wins tied best record for 1954–55 season.

Winningest NBL/NBA Fort Wayne Coaches during entire history of the franchise:
>   **Charley Eckman**...................................123
>   Paul Birch...105
>   Murray Mendenhall 72
>   Carl Bennett 58
>   Bob McDermott 43

Winningest NBA Fort Wayne/Detroit Pistons:
Chuck Daley ....538 (9 seasons)
Ray Scott 147
Charley Eckman 123
Dick McGuire 122
Paul Birch 105

Piston Coach Most Times in the NBA Finals:
Chuck Daly 3
Charley Eckman 2

Piston Coach Most Times Finishing First in Division:
Chuck Daly 3
Charley Eckman 3*
Tied for first in 1956–57 season

ZOLLNER
ZOLLNER MACHINE WORKS
PISTONS

BUETER ROAD
FORT WAYNE 4, INDIANA

CONTRACT AGREEMENT

THIS AGREEMENT, made and entered into by and between ZOLLNER MACHINE WORKS, INC., a Minnesota corporation, owner of the Zollner Piston Professional Basketball Team, hereinafter referred to as "Zollner", and CHARLES M. ECKMAN, hereinafter referred to as "Eckman", WITNESSETH:

Zollner wishes to employ Eckman as Piston Basketball Coach and Eckman wishes to accept this position under the following terms and conditions:

Authority. Eckman is to be coach and have full charge of team operation and will be responsible only to Zollner's President. Zollner's President is to establish all general policy regulations, which will specifically include approval by the President of all player contract transactions.

Work Year. Eckman is to devote his full time to Piston Basketball. In between seasons he is to do whatever is necessary for the general welfare of the Piston Basketball operation.

Compensation. Eckman is to receive a basic salary of Ten Thousand Dollars ($10,000) per annum, and subject to the following bonuses:

One Thousand Dollars ($1,000) for team finish in play-off bracket;
One Thousand Dollars ($1,000) for team win in each play-off series if three (3) series are scheduled; if only two (2) series are required for championship, Fifteen Hundred Dollars ($1,500) per series win.

Eckman specifically waives right to participate in players' play-off pool.

Term. The term of this contract shall be for two (2) years during the period from April 20, 1954 to April 20, 1956.

Salary Payment. Eckman is to be paid the sum of Four Hundred Dollars ($400) on April 20, 1954, and Eight Hundred Dollars ($800) per month on a twelve-months basis.

IN WITNESS WHEREOF, the parties hereto have hereunto set their hands and seals, this 19th day of April, 1954.

ZOLLNER MACHINE WORKS, INC.

ACCEPTED:

By _____
President

_____
Charles M. Eckman

"Experience Counts"

Charley's original contract with the Fort Wayne Zollner Pistons, 1954-56.

National League of Professional Baseball Clubs

UNIFORM EMPLOYE'S CONTRACT

Parties The .... **MILWAUKEE BRAVES, INC.** ....

herein called the Club, and .... **CHARLES ECKMAN** ....

of .... **GLEN BURNIE, MARYLAND** ...., herein called the Employe.

Recital The Club is a member of the National League of Professional Baseball Clubs. As such, and jointly with the other members of the League, it is a party to agreements and rules with the American League of Professional Baseball Clubs and its constituent clubs, and with the National Association of Professional Baseball Leagues. The purpose of these agreements and rules is to insure to the public wholesome and high-class professional baseball by defining the relations between clubs and their employes, between club and club, between league and league, and by vesting in a designated League President and Commissioner broad powers of control and discipline, and of decision in case of disputes.

Agreement In view of the facts above recited the parties agree as follows:

Employment 1. The Club hereby employs the Employe to render skilled service as a baseball .... **SCOUT** .... *
in connection with all baseball activities of the Club during the year......19..**63**.. and the Employe covenants that he will perform with diligence and fidelity the service stated and such duties as may be required of him by the Club.

Salary 2. For the service aforesaid the Club will pay the Employe an aggregate salary of $.**3,000.00**........
..........**(Three Thousand Dollars)**.............., payable as follows:**

To be paid in six (6) equal installments, April thru September, 1963.

Loyalty 3. (a) The Employe shall faithfully serve the Club, and pledges himself to the American public to conform to high standards of personal conduct, of fair play and good sportsmanship.
(b) The Employe represents that he does not, directly or indirectly, own stock or have any financial interest in the ownership or earnings of any Major League club, except as hereinafter expressly set forth, and covenants that he will not hereafter, while connected with any Major League club, acquire or hold any such stock or interest except in accordance with Major League Rule 20 (e).

Service 4. The Employe shall not render baseball service during the period of this contract otherwise than for the Club.

Termination 5. This contract may be terminated at any time by the Club upon ten days' written notice to the Employe.

Regulations 6. The Employe accepts as part of this contract such reasonable regulations as the Club may announce from time to time.

* Insert *coach, scout, trainer*, etc., as case may be.
** State how salary is to be paid, including date of commencement or period within which payments are to be made.

Charley's 1963 National League contract with the Milwaukee Braves as a baseball scout.

The Eckman Lexicon

An Authority is a guy from out-of-town.

An Expert (see an Authority).

"Ain't No Way" translates to "No matter what you have been led to believe in this matter or assumed, that facts indicate there is not a snowball's chance in hell that what you believe is actually true."

"A Yo-Yo!" is a guy who goes up and down but don't go nowhere.

"Bawlemore" is the name of the Queen City of the Patapsco River drainage area located in the State of Maryland.

"Better than the movies!" translates to "Hollywood script writers could not concoct a scenario this wild or funny."

"Call a cab!" means "The time has come for this conversation between us to come to an end and for you to head in a different direction."

"Call two cabs!" means "The time has come for this conversation between us to come to an end because you are an idiot and no matter what direction you head, you are still wrong!"

(Please note the subtle difference between the two expressions involving the command of calling a taxi.)

MOOSE

As appeared in the News American, *April 19, 1978.*

"It's a very simple game!" denotes that so called experts are attempting to describe a situation with complex theories that are so much horse manure *(and Charley smelled horse manure from wherever it emanated)* when, in fact, the explanation could not be plainer.

"Like Halloween and New Year's Eve on the same night" means the events that transpired had a surrealistic quality that accompanies an extraordinary event or celebration that is rarely seen more than once a year but is something truly memorable when it does occur.

"O–O–O–rioles" *(pronounced OOOOOH–rioles)* is a major league baseball team that plays in Bawlemore. *(For an explanation of Bawlemore see above.)*

"Rompin' and a Stompin'" translates to "an individual in authority who is putting on an extreme show of emotion on the sideline of an athletic contest, or, when applied to a horse race, a thoroughbred that is running very fast approaching the finish line." *(The latter was an event that did not happen as often as Charley would have liked.)*

"The old federal case" means either to make something big out of nothing or the IRS is looking into your back taxes.

"You can give 'em the saliva test!" means that the person who has conveyed that bit of information to you has a few bricks less than a full load and should live in a padded cell.

"You can go to sleep on them cherries!" translates to "This is the truth, the whole truth and nothing but the truth and if you disagree you should take the saliva test."

As appeared in the News American, *November 20, 1974.*

MOOSE MILLER

MAR 15, 1980

HELLO CHARLIE —

THE ORIOLES MANAGEMENT MUST BE
NUTS FOR NOT MAKING YOU A REGULAR
MEMBER of THEIR ANNOUNCING TEAM
THEY NEED YOU!!

P.S. THIS CARTOON WILL APPEAR IN THE
NEWS-AMERICAN ON TUESDAY MARCH 18TH

ALL THE BEST
BOB WEBER